Table of Contents

Staff

Senior Vice President, Publisher,
Adult Trade and Reference
Bruce Nichols

Vice President,
Executive Editor
Joseph P. Pickett

Vice President,
Managing Editor
Christopher Leonesio

Project Editor
Peter Chipman

Consulting Editor
David Pritchard

Database Production
Supervisor
Christopher Granniss

Editor
Catherine T. Pratt

Art and Production
Supervisor
Margaret Anne Miles

Editorial and Production Coordinator
Sarah Iani

Illustrator
Nancy Grunthaner Meyers

Text Design
Edda Sigurđardóttir, PORT Design

Preface

This book is set up not as a textbook or workbook but as a handy reference guide to the most common grammatical terms. Its alphabetical arrangement allows you to look up words directly, without first having to consult an index in the back of the book. We hope that you will find the dictionary useful over the course of many years of study—starting with very basic concepts like *noun* or *subject* and running all the way through *correlative conjunction* and *demonstrative* to advanced concepts like *predicate nominative* and *subjunctive conditional.*

How to Use this Book

The dictionary is arranged alphabetically. Most entries begin with an example sentence, which is followed by an explanation of the grammatical feature in question. Occasionally, one of the words in the definition will be printed in **boldface**—this is meant to tell you that we strongly suggest that you look up the word in question if you don't already know it.

In addition to the main definition and explanation of the word, most entries include at least one of these special features:

- **Other examples** help to illustrate the concept explained in the definition. In these example sentences, we often use *italic* letters to draw your attention to specific parts of the example that the entry word relates to. Sometimes, when we also want to draw your attention to some other grammatical feature in the example sentence, we use both italics (for the feature we're talking about) and underlining (for the other feature).

- **Exceptions** only appear in a few entries, to let you know about a few ways that grammar doesn't always follow the rules we're telling you about.

- **Cautions** are warnings, especially about ways of using language that many people consider to be mistakes, such as relying too much on the passive voice.

- **Useful tips** can serve several purposes. They can provide advice on punctuation or other aspects of sentence mechanics, as in the tips at *contraction*. They can offer information on dictionary use, as in the tip at *part of speech*. Or they can help clarify grammatical points that many people find confusing, as in the tip at *phrase*.

- **See also** tells you where to look to learn about other words that are closely related. Most entries list at least one **See also** word.

If you're uncertain about how to pronounce any of the grammatical terms listed in the dictionary, turn to page 151 for a pronunciation guide.

A

absolute construction

Honestly, there's a hornet on your back.

An absolute construction is a part of a sentence that has no direct connection to the words or phrases in the rest of the sentence. Rather, absolute constructions modify the sentence as a whole. For example, in the sentence above, the adverb *honestly* is an absolute construction. It doesn't modify any verb or adjective or other adverb in the sentence; it just means that the speaker is being honest (or claiming to be honest, anyway).

An absolute construction can be a single word, as in the example above, or it can be a phrase, as in the sentence "*Generally speaking,* I'm in bed by 9:30." Absolute constructions are often placed at the beginning of a sentence, but they can occur at the end or in the middle, too.

■ **Other examples:** "*Unfortunately*, we're all out of bread."

"I don't know you that well, but *for what it's worth*, I think you're nice."

"There's no school tomorrow, *it being a state holiday*."

■ **Useful tip:** Some grammar books refer to constructions that consist of a single adverb modifying the whole sentence as "sentence adverbs" instead of "absolute constructions." They apply the term "absolute construction" only to constructions that include a noun, a participle, and any associated objects and modifiers, as in the sentence "*The stairs being rather steep*, I had to use the handrail."

■ **Caution:** The word *hopefully* often appears as an absolute construction, in sentences like "*Hopefully* you remembered to bring an umbrella." Many people (including some teachers) consider this particular absolute construction to be a mistake, although they don't usually object to similar instances such as "*Thankfully*, no one was injured."

See also: dangling modifier

abstract noun

Nouns come in two basic types—concrete and abstract. Abstract nouns, like *hope, enthusiasm, deliciousness, reality,* and *complication,* don't refer directly to objects, people, or events. Many abstract nouns, like *memory* or *anticipation,* have to do with people's thoughts, feelings, or personalities. Others, like *wetness* or *angle,* have to do with the qualities of real-world objects. Still others, like *democracy* and *zoology,* are used to name the general ideas and categories we use in making sense of life.

Even the title is abstract!

■ **Useful tip:** Many abstract nouns can be used in either of two ways, either generally or specifically. For instance, you can use the abstract noun *friendship* without any articles or modifiers to refer to the idea of having friends ("*Friendship* is very important to me"). Or you can use it with one or more articles or modifiers to refer to a specific relationship between one friend and another ("This is the beginning of a beautiful *friendship*").

See also: concrete noun

action verb

An action verb, such as *walk, shrink, pay, calculate,* or *smash,* is any verb that describes an action or occurrence—whether in the past, present, or future, whether in the real world or some completely made-up situation.

- **Caution:** Sometimes the "action" described by an action verb doesn't seem like much of an action at all. *Wait* is an action verb, for instance. So is *rest.* So are *forget, owe, sit,* and *stagnate.* So don't let the term "action verb" confuse you. It really refers to any verb you can think of that isn't an auxiliary or a linking verb.

- **Useful tip:** To make your writing as lively and interesting as possible, make sure you don't rely too much on linking verbs. This paragraph uses nothing but linking verbs:

  Yesterday <u>was</u> my birthday. My birthday present from my parents <u>was</u> a rafting trip down Red Canyon. The canyon <u>is</u> ten miles long. My guests <u>were</u> Aaron, Ramón, and Omar. The trip <u>was</u> scary but exciting.

  This paragraph uses a variety of action verbs:

  Yesterday, for my birthday, my parents <u>treated</u> me to a rafting trip. Aaron, Ramón, and Omar <u>joined</u> us. As we <u>paddled</u> down ten-mile-long Red Canyon, my pulse <u>raced</u> with fear and excitement.

See also: auxiliary verb, linking verb

active voice

Weasels dislike strawberries.

The active voice is one of the two grammatical **voices** in English. Most ordinary sentences, like the example above, or "We *left* home in a big hurry," or "The earth *rotates* on its axis once a day," are in the active voice. That means that the agent—the person or thing performing the action in the sentence—is also the grammatical subject. (In the examples above, the weasels are the ones disliking strawberries, we are the ones leaving in a hurry, and the earth is the one rotating.)

People use the active voice most of the time when speaking, without really thinking about it. It's a good idea to use it most of the time when writing, too, since it's the most straightforward way to set up a sentence and since it clearly communicates who is doing what.

■ **Caution:** The term "active voice," like the term "action verb," can be confusing. It has to do with the way the grammar of the sentence is set up, not with whether the verb in the sentence is describing energetic or lively events. The sentence "I took a nap" is in the active voice. So is the sentence "She said nothing all afternoon."

■ **Useful tip:** In some sentences, using the active voice isn't the best choice—particularly when the person or thing that you're most interested in is the one that something happens to, not the one that's doing something. In cases like that, it often makes more sense to use the other grammatical voice—the passive. For example, saying "Our house was struck by lightning" (passive voice) puts more emphasis on the danger to the house and the people inside, whereas "Lightning struck our house" (active voice) puts more emphasis on the lightning.

See also: agent, passive voice, logical subject

adjectival noun

Youth is wasted on the young.

An adjectival noun is a word that would ordinarily be an adjective but acts as a noun, like the word *young* in the saying above. Most of the time when a sentence includes an adjectival noun, it's easy to tell from the context that the adjectival noun actually stands for a longer phrase—in this case "young people" or "people who are young."

In terms of their grammar, adjectival nouns work pretty much just like other nouns. They can fill any of these roles:

● grammatical subjects ("The *best* is yet to come")
● objects of verbs ("I try to think the *best* of my friends")
● objects of prepositions ("Let's hope for the *best*").

But there's one big difference—with adjectival nouns, there's usually no difference between their singular and plural forms. For instance, *best* can be a singular adjectival noun ("I'd like a new scarf, please—only the *best* will do"). Or it can be plural ("I'd like seventeen new scarves, please—only the *best* will do").

■ **Other examples:** "Only the *strong* survive."

"Sort through the apples, separating the *good* from the *bad*."

"Give me the *largest* you have."

"Emma was the *first* to cross the finish line."

adjective

Adjectives, such as *hollow, funny, sweeter, rough,* and *greatest,* are one of the **parts of speech.** They usually act as **modifiers**—that is, they add to the meaning or change the meaning of other words—in this case, nouns. Most of the time an adjective will appear just before the noun it's describing, as the adjective *dark* does in the phrase "a dark night" or *embarrassing* does in "an embarrassing mistake."

When the meaning of the sentence calls for it, a single noun can be modified by more than one adjective, as in the phrase "*a large, scaly, sharp-fanged snake.*" If you've spoken English your whole life, you probably already know what order to put these adjectives in without even thinking about it. However, if English is your second language, it may take some effort to learn the order (or "hierarchy") of adjectives that makes sense to English speakers.

Sometimes one little adjective makes all the difference.

▪ **Useful tip:** In writing, it's traditional to put commas between adjectives when you have several of them in a row. The usual guideline is this: If it would sound OK in speech to stick an *and* between the adjectives, it's OK to use a comma between them in writing. For example, if in speaking you might talk about having "a *long* and *heartfelt* conversation," then it would also be acceptable to write it with a comma in place of the *and*: "a *long, heartfelt* conversation."

See also: adjectival noun, adjective complement, appositive adjective, attributive adjective, degree, hierarchy of adjectives, indefinite adjective, predicate adjective, proper adjective, verbal adjective

adjective complement

The city is full of cars and people.

An adjective complement is an adverbial phrase or clause that helps clarify the meaning of a particular adjective in a sentence. For instance, if you just tell someone "The city is full," they have no idea what the city is full of. Adding an adjective complement helps to clarify what you meant by the adjective *full*. Perhaps the city is full *of zombies*! Or maybe it's just full *of cars and people.*

▪ **Other examples:** "I'm sorry *that I hurt your feelings.*"

"That piece of pizza is too big *for you to fit all of it in your mouth all at one time.*"

"He was unable *to explain the meaning of my dream.*"

See also: adverbial clause, adverbial phrase, compound complement

adverb

Never forget to zip up your backpack!

Adverbs, such as *always, upwards, softly, easily, anyhow,* and *then,* are one of the **parts of speech.** They are usually used to modify verbs, as in the phrases "*never* forget," "dance *well,*" and "stir *quickly.*"

Adverbs usually help provide the following information:

● *why* or *how* something is done ("The raccoon ate *greedily*")
● *to what extent* something happens ("Watch out! You *nearly* knocked me over!")
● *where* or *when* something happens ("Come *here*! Do it *now*!").

In addition to modifying verbs, adverbs can also modify adjectives, as in the phrases "*more* successful," "*incredibly* embarrassing," or "*surprisingly* deep." Or they can modify other adverbs, as the adverb *very* does in the phrase "*very* simply." Sometimes an adverb is even used to modify an entire sentence ("*Unfortunately,* my dog ate my homework").

- **Caution:** Many adverbs end with the suffix *–ly*, which makes it easy to recognize them. But a lot of important adverbs, like *well* and *never*, don't end in *–ly*, and a lot of words that do end in *–ly* aren't adverbs—like *friendly, silly,* and *ugly.* So you can't rely on the spelling to tell you whether a word is an adverb or not. Instead, try to figure out what it's modifying. If the word or phrase being modified is a verb, an adjective, or an adverb, then the modifier must be an adverb.

See also: adverbial, adverbial clause, adverbial phrase, conjunctive adverb

adverbial clause

Max sneezed because he's allergic to cats.

An adverbial clause is a whole **subordinate clause** that acts as an adverb in the grammar of a sentence. For example, in the sentence above, the clause "because he's allergic to cats" works like an adverb to modify the verb *sneezed*—to tell *why* Max sneezed.

- **Other examples:** "I often sing *when I am in the shower.*" (modifies the verb *sing*)

  "I parked my bike *where I always do.*" (modifies the verb *parked*)

  "She frowned *as if she didn't remember me.*" (modifies the verb *frowned*)

- **Useful tip:** Most of the time, an adverbial clause follows the verb it's modifying—or follows the object of the verb, if the verb takes a direct object. Sometimes, an adverbial clause will appear at the beginning of a sentence, before the grammatical subject ("*When the doors opened,* everyone ran to get the best seats"). But it's very rare for an adverbial clause to appear between the subject and the verb or between the verb and a direct object.

- **Useful tip:** Adverbial clauses don't always modify verbs. Sometimes they modify adjectives, as in the sentence "I was nervous *when I saw the alligator I had offered to wrestle.*" In cases like this, the clause is called an **adjective complement**.

See also: adverbial phrase

adverbial phrase

Jasmine reached for the paddle.

An adverbial phrase is a group of two or more words that act together in the grammar of a sentence as if they were a single adverb. For example, in the sentence above, the prepositional phrase "for the paddle" acts like an adverb to modify the verb *reached*, telling us the reason why Jasmine reached.

Adverbial phrases don't have to be prepositional phrases. They can also be participial phrases, as in the sentence "Vladimir lay *stretched out comfortably on the couch*," where the participial phrase modifies the verb *lay*, telling us about how Vladimir was lying. Or they can be infinitive phrases, as in the sentence "Emma coughed *to signal me to stop talking before I embarrassed myself*," where the infinitive phrase modifies the verb *coughed*, telling about the reason why Emma was coughing.

■ **Useful tip:** Adverbial phrases don't always modify verbs. Sometimes they modify adjectives, as in the sentence "Early in the morning, the grass was still wet *with dew*." In cases like this, the phrase is called an **adjective complement**.

See also: adverbial clause, infinitive phrase, participial phrase, prepositional phrase

affix

An affix consists of one or more syllables, like *re–* or *–ful*, that can be attached to the beginning or the end of a word (or to a **stem**) to produce a new word with a different but related meaning. Adding an affix to a word may or may not change the part of speech the word belongs to. For example, adding the prefix *mis–* to the verb *count* gives another verb, *miscount*. However, adding the suffix *–able* to the same verb gives an adjective, *countable*.

■ **Other examples:** *inter–* as in *interactive* or *interstate*
  sub– as in *submarine, subtitle,* or *subway*
  un– as in *unfold, unmask,* or *unlikely*
  –ify as in *fortify, justify,* or *personify*
  –able as in *adaptable, erasable,* or *lovable*
  –ed as in *climbed, grabbed,* or *invented*

- **Useful tip:** Because the same affixes reappear so frequently with the same meaning in so many words—as in *rethink, reword, rewrite*, and so on—anyone who grows up speaking English already has a good idea of what many of the most common affixes mean. So the people who write dictionaries don't bother to include every possible word that could be formed with every possible affix. You won't find *prefried* in most dictionaries, but since you know the meaning of *fried* and you know the meaning of the affix *pre–*, you're unlikely to be confused when you're shopping in the supermarket and you spot a package of something claiming to be *prefried bacon*.

See also: prefix, suffix

agent

The lead guitarist smashed his guitar after the final song.

The agent is the one that's actually doing something in the situation described by a verb. Most of the time the agent is also the grammatical subject, as *guitarist* is in the sentence above. However, when a sentence has a passive verb, the agent is placed in a prepositional phrase beginning with *by* ("The guitar was smashed *by the lead guitarist* after the final song") or in some cases may not appear in the sentence at all ("The guitar was smashed after the final song").

In sentences with more than one verb, there may be a single agent for more than one verb ("*She* <u>dove</u> to the left, <u>fielded</u> the grounder, and <u>threw</u> the runner out at first base"). Or there may be a different agent for each verb ("*Vlad* <u>told</u> me that *you* <u>fell</u> in the river").

- **Caution:** Outside of discussions of grammar, *agent* most often means "a person with the power or authority to act for another." Don't be misled by this everyday meaning into assuming that the agent in a sentence will always be a person. Sometimes the agent is a physical object ("*The raindrops* fell quietly on the lawn") or even an abstract idea ("*Happiness* means different things to different people").

See also: active voice, grammatical subject, logical subject, passive voice

agreement

In everyday life, you have an "agreement" when two or more people say or feel the same thing. In grammar, "agreement" has a somewhat similar meaning: two or more parts of the sentence are in agreement when their grammatical forms match each other in some way. Some languages have a lot of different kinds of agreement, but in English there are only a few kinds of grammatical agreement that you need to watch out for:

- First, the subject of a clause should always "agree" with the verb in terms of **person** and **number**. For instance, if the grammatical subject is the second-person pronoun *you*, the verb also has to be a second-person form like *take* or *give*, not a third-person form like *takes* or *gives*. (This is why a sentence like "You gives me a canteloupe" is wrong.) If the grammatical subject is a plural noun like *bumblebees*, the verb also has to be a plural form like *swarm* or *sting*, not a singular verb like *swarms* or *stings*. (You wouldn't say "Seventeen bumblebees stings Max.")

- Second, when you use a number as an adjective to modify a noun, the noun should be singular if the number is one and plural if the number is more than one. You would say "one bumblebee," but "seventeen bumblebee*s*." Some other words also need to agree with the noun they modify: *each*, *every*, *that*, and *this* modify singular nouns, while *all*, *both*, *few*, *many*, *most*, *several*, *these*, and *those* modify plural nouns.

Useful tip: It's sometimes hard to get the agreement between subject and verb right when the subject is modified with added phrases. For instance, the singular noun *woman* should always take a singular verb ("The *woman* waves and says hello"). Attaching a phrase like "with the three poodles" to the subject doesn't change the number of the subject—it's still the woman who is waving and saying hello, so the verb still needs to be singular no matter how many poodles she has ("The *woman* with the three poodles waves and says hello").

antecedent

I have tried liverwurst, and I can't stand it.

The antecedent of a pronoun is the person, place, thing, or idea that the pronoun stands for in a particular sentence. For instance, in the sentence "You play a kazoo by humming into it," the pronoun *it* stands for "a kazoo," so we would say that "a kazoo" is the antecedent of the pronoun *it* in this sentence. If you're writing or speaking clearly, your readers or listeners should be able to figure out the antecedent of each pronoun without much trouble—usually because the antecedent has already been mentioned by name.

- **Other examples:** "I have tried *liverwurst*, and I can't stand *it*."

  "Next time I see *Emma*, I'm going to tell *her* what I really think of *her* liverwurst sandwiches."

  "The female *turtle* returns to the sea once *she* has laid *her* eggs in the sand."

- **Caution:** If you use similar pronouns more than once in a sentence to refer to different antecedents, you run the risk of causing confusion. If someone says that "Vlad told Max *he'd* beaten *him* in the essay contest," how are you supposed to know which pronoun stands for Vlad and which stands for Max? And even if there's only one pronoun in a sentence, there's room for confusion if the sentence includes more than one possible antecedent: If you hear that "Max told Vlad *he'd* won the essay contest," who won the contest? Max? Or Vlad?

- **Useful tip:** The antecedent of the pronouns *I* and *me* is always the speaker, and the antecedent of *you* is always the person being spoken to. The antecedent of *we* and *us* includes the speaker, but it may or may not include the person being spoken to. That's why, if your friend runs into a room and yells "Great news! *We're* going to Bermuda!" you shouldn't run off to begin packing your beach towels until you find out just who *we* are. With any luck, it will include you (the one being spoken to) as well as your friend (the speaker); if not, maybe you'll get a postcard.

See also: anticipatory subject

anticipatory subject

It is important not to leave the cage door open.

In the sentence above, the word *it* is called an anticipatory subject. That's because *it* is acting as the grammatical subject of the sentence and because the antecedent of *it*—in this case, "not to leave the cage door open"—doesn't appear until later in the sentence. Just as a person anticipating a future event is looking forward to that event,

a pronoun that acts as an anticipatory subject is looking forward toward an antecedent that will appear later on in the sentence.

- **Other examples:** "*It* feels good *having my back scratched.*"

  "*It* is hard *to balance a canteloupe on an egg.*"

  "*It* amazed me *that you knew the answer.*"

appositive

The platypus, an animal native to Australia, is one of the few egg-laying mammals.

An appositive, a kind of **parenthetical expression**, is a noun phrase that follows immediately after another noun phrase, clarifying it or adding a little more information about it. For instance, the phrase "an animal native to Australia" is an appositive in the sentence above, adding a little more information about the platypus. An appositive isn't grammatically connected to the rest of the sentence, so usually it's set off from the rest of the sentence with commas immediately before and after it.

- **Other examples:** "Phoenix, *the capital of Arizona,* is very hot in the summer."

  "Thomas Jefferson, *the third president,* served two terms."

  "I found myself locked in the cellar, *a dark, foul-smelling place with cobwebs dangling from the ceiling and slimy water seeping from the brick walls.*"

See also: appositive adjective

appositive adjective

The pigeons, attracted by the breadcrumbs, fluttered all around the man on the bench.

Like an appositive, an appositive adjective immediately follows a noun or noun phrase, clarifying it or adding a little more information about it. But unlike an ordinary appositive, an appositive adjective doesn't act like a noun. You might guess from its name that an appositive adjective is a kind of adjective. And you'd be right—partly. But an appositive adjective isn't always a single word. It can also take the form of a phrase— such as the participial phrase "attracted by breadcrumbs" in the sentence above—that acts like an adjective to modify the previous noun phrase.

- **Other examples:** "Emma, *undiscouraged*, tried once again to bake brownies without burning them."

  "Jasmine, *helpful as ever*, took the brownies out of the oven just in time."

  "The smoke detector, *responding to the particles of burnt brownie in the air*, began to beep loudly."

- **Useful tip:** Single-word appositive adjectives sometimes appear without commas before and after them—especially in older songs or poems, which might refer to "rivers *wide* and mountains *high*" or to "a maiden *fair*." But if you use this construction in ordinary writing or speech, people are probably going to think you sound weird and old-fashioned. It's probably best to avoid it most of the time.

See also: appositive, attributive adjective, parenthetical expression

article

Articles, like *a, an,* and *the,* are one of the **parts of speech.** They're used before nouns or at the beginning of noun phrases, and they help to explain how the thing named by the noun relates to the overall category of things it belongs to. For instance, if you just use a noun by itself with no article at all, you signal to your reader that you're thinking of the noun in very general terms: "*Light* travels at 180,000 miles per second." If you use a noun with the indefinite article *a* or *an*, it means that the noun refers to one of several possible things of its kind: "We were crawling through the cave when we suddenly saw a *light*." And if you use the definite article *the*, it means that you're referring to one specific thing: "*The light* in the refrigerator won't turn on."

- **Useful tip:** Most proper nouns name one-of-a-kind things. They don't name a whole category of things, so there's no need to use an article to show whether you're referring to them in general or specific terms. Nobody would say "My English teacher is *an Alexandra Wilhelmina Throckmorton*" or "Someday I'd like to travel to *the Beijing, China.*" You only need to use an article for names like these when the name might refer to any of several people or things: "You mean you're <u>the</u> *Sue Smith*? The one who broke the world speed record for unicycle riding?"

See also: definite article, determiner, indefinite article

aspect

The aspect of a verb is a way of describing how the verb's action is experienced in time. But it's different from **tense**, which also has to do with time. Every verb or verb phrase has a tense, of course, which tells whether the action of the clause takes place in the past, the present, or the future. But many verbs also have an aspect, which tells whether the action simply happens, has already been completed, or is still going on <u>at the point in time the clause is talking about, not necessarily at the present moment.</u> This last detail is important! For example, the sentences "I *have finished* the book" and "I *will have finished* the book by the time we have class tomorrow" both have the same aspect (the "perfect" aspect) because they both describe a point in time when your reading of the book is completed—even though in the first sentence that time is now and in the second sentence that time hasn't come yet.

The prosecutor covers every aspect of the case—grammatical or otherwise!

The different aspects of a verb are signaled both by changing the verb itself and by adding particular auxiliary verbs such as *be* and *have*.

- **Examples:** "I *ride* a camel."

  "I *am riding* a camel."

  "I *have ridden* a camel."

See also: habitual aspect, perfect aspect, progressive aspect, simple tense

attributive adjective

An attributive adjective, like the word *fortunate* in the phrase "a *fortunate* coincidence," is one that directly modifies a noun, forming a part of a larger noun phrase. In English, attributive adjectives are placed immediately before the noun they modify.

▨ **Examples:** "a *terrible* drought"

"my *best* friend"

"*tiny, delicate, six-sided* snowflakes"

▨ **Exception:** There are a handful of English adjectives that usually come after the noun they modify. *Junior* and *senior* are used this way when they modify a proper name. *Aplenty* and *galore* always follow the noun they modify too. So do adjectives that have been borrowed into English from languages like French or Spanish (both of which often put adjectives after nouns), like *extraordinaire* in the phrase "a musician *extraordinaire*" or *grande* in the term "taco *grande*."

See also: appositive adjective, attributive noun, predicate adjective

attributive noun

A noun that is used as an attributive adjective, like the word *city* in the phrase "city bus" or *airplane* in "airplane wing," is called an attributive noun. Many nouns in English can act as attributive nouns. They're different from regular adjectives because they usually can't be modified by adverbs (you could say "a very *narrow wing*" but you wouldn't say "a very airplane wing") or be used as subject complements (you could say "that wing is *narrow*" but you wouldn't say "that wing is airplane").

▨ **Other examples:** "a *shovel* handle"

"a *hotel* lobby"

"a *movie* star"

See also: attributive adjective

auxiliary verb

An auxiliary verb is a verb that works along with the main verb to help express a slightly different meaning than the main verb would have if it were used on its own. Auxiliaries can serve various purposes:

- They can help describe something as happening in the future, like the *will* in "will go." (See future tense.)

- They can help tell whether a particular action was already finished by some point in time, like the *had* in "had washed." (See aspect.)

- They can make it clear that a particular action is possible, allowed, or required, or that the sentence is describing something that didn't actually happen, like the *should* in "should have asked." (See modal verb.)

- They can make it clear that something or someone undergoes a particular action, like the *was* in "was ridden." (See passive voice.)

- The verb *do* serves as an auxiliary verb when we ask questions ("Do you want some of my orange?") or give sentences a negative meaning ("I don't like tuna").

Auxiliary verbs are placed before the main verb of the verb phrase. If there's more than one auxiliary verb in the verb phrase, only the first one is a finite verb—that is, it's the only one that gets inflected based on the number and person of the grammatical subject—and in fact, many of the auxiliary verbs have only one form, so they don't change to reflect differences in number or person even when they come first in the phrase. As for the main verb, if you attach auxiliaries to it, it doesn't get inflected for person or number either, though it may sometimes be changed to a past or present participle form to help express grammatical aspect or voice.

> **Useful tip:** The word *auxiliary* means "giving help," so you can see why these verbs are called auxiliary verbs—they help the main verb to express a particular meaning that it can't express on its own. In fact, auxiliary verbs are often called "helping verbs."

See also: finite verb, inflection, mood, verb phrase

bare infinitive

Some migrating birds can fly thousands of miles without stopping.

The bare infinitive of a verb is the form it appears under when you look it up in the dictionary. The verbs *fly, knock, giggle,* and *demolish,* for example, are all bare infinitives; *flew, knocks, giggled,* and *demolishing* aren't.

- Whenever the main verb of a verb phrase follows a modal verb like *can* or *should,* the main verb appears in the bare infinitive form.

- The bare infinitive form is also the verb form used in all imperative sentences.

The bare infinitive of a verb is identical to the ordinary present-tense verb forms for everything except the third-person singular, which is formed by adding *–s* or *–es* to the bare infinitive.

- **Exception:** The bare infinitive of the verb *be* is different from all of its present-tense forms ("I *am,*" "you *are,*" "it *was,*" "we *were,*" "you were," "they *were*").

- **Useful tip:** The bare infinitive is also used in constructions like "I saw Max *eat* the last three brownies" or "I felt something *touch* my arm." There are only a small number of verbs that can appear as the main verb in constructions like these—aside from *see* and *feel,* the list includes *hear* ("I heard her *giggle* when I slipped and fell,"), *watch* ("I watched the egg *hit* the floor and *smash*"), *let* ("Don't let the brownies *burn*!"), *make* ("The teacher made him *read* his essay aloud"), and a few others.

See also: finite verb, infinitive

C

cardinal number

All seven sheep walked into the lion's den.

The cardinal numbers are
the numbers that you use in
counting or measuring—*one,
two, three, seventy-five,* and
so on. Cardinal numbers can
act grammatically either as
adjectives ("All *seven* sheep
walked into the lion's den") or
as nouns ("Only *six* walked out").

When you're using a cardinal number larger than one as the grammatical subject of a clause, it takes a singular verb if you're talking about the number as a number ("*Thirteen is* my lucky number"), but it takes a plural verb if it stands for a particular number of something ("Of the nineteen kids in the class, *thirteen are* girls").

■ **Useful tip:** Cardinal numbers can either be spelled out or written using numerals. If you're only writing about a few numbers, and if those numbers are fairly small, it's traditional to spell them out: "We'll be camping at the pond for *three* days." But if some of the numbers you're writing about are larger numbers, it's a good idea to use numerals: "Of the *49,420* people living in Whipple City, only *9* play the banjo."

See also: ordinal number

case

In some languages, the grammatical structure of a sentence is shown almost entirely by changes to the form of individual words, which get **inflections** depending on what role they play in a sentence. When a noun acts as the grammatical subject it will have a different form than it has when it's used as a direct object, and it will have yet another form if it's used as an indirect object. Likewise, the pronouns, articles, and even adjectives change their form in these languages, to match the nouns.

The different grammatical roles that the word forms show are called cases. Some languages have lots of them, but English has only a few.

- We show ownership or other relationships by using case endings on nouns (we say "*Leon's* toothbrush" or "*Leon's* friend," not "*Leon* toothbrush" or "*Leon* friend") or by using special sets of pronouns (*my, your, their,* etc.)

- We also have different sets of pronouns to show whether something or someone is the subject or object of a clause (we say "*I* pinched my brother," but "My brother pinched *me* back," not "My brother pinched *I* back").

See also: genitive, objective (pronoun), subjective (pronoun)

clause

The sun rose like a glowing coal over the palm-fringed lagoon.

Clauses are the basic building blocks of sentences. Every complete sentence has at least one clause, and many sentences have two or more. No matter how complicated a sentence may seem, it can always be broken down into a series of clauses that work together to get the meaning across. At its simplest, a clause consists of a **subject** and a **predicate**, with the predicate always containing at least one **finite verb**. For example, the sentence "The sun rose like a glowing coal over the palm-fringed lagoon" is a single clause. Its subject is "The sun" and its predicate is "rose like a glowing coal over the palm-fringed lagoon." The finite verb in the predicate is *rose,* the past tense of *rise.*

Not all clauses are created equal, though. Some (**independent clauses**) can stand by themselves as a complete sentence, as in the example above. Others (**subordinate clauses**) can only exist as part of sentences that also have at least one independent clause.

- **Other examples:** "when *Emma arrived*"

  "my *nose is* itchy"

  "no *penguin can* fly"

  "if *you* don't *help* me"

  "because *ketchup*, of all the ingredients in the kitchen, including cinnamon, mayonnaise, and frozen peas, *tastes* the worst mixed into brownies"

- **Caution:** Participles and infinitives look a lot like verbs, and sometimes they're described as being forms of verbs, but they don't count toward making a clause be a clause—only finite verbs do. "The man *looking* for his hat" is not a clause, though "The man *looks* for his hat" is, and so is

"The man *was* looking for his hat." Likewise, "to *slide* down the banister" is not a clause, but "She *likes* to slide down the banister" is.

See also: compound-complex sentence, compound sentence, complex sentence, conditional clause, coordinate clause, main clause, nominal clause, nonrestrictive clause, relative clause, restrictive clause, simple sentence

collective noun

The team has a few very good players.

A collective noun, like the word *team* in the sentence above, is a noun that's grammatically singular but stands for a group of people or things. (Actually, *group* is a collective noun too!) In a sentence where a collective noun is the grammatical subject, it will usually get matched with a singular verb—like the word *has* in the sentence above.

■ **Other examples:** "A *pack* of wolves *is* approaching."

"My *collection contains* some very rare coins."

"The *deck* of cards *is* missing the two of hearts."

■ **Useful tip:** Though collective nouns themselves are grammatically singular, a pronoun or possessive adjective standing for a collective noun can be either singular or plural, depending on whether it refers more to the group as a group or to the individual members of the group. For instance, it would be correct to say "My *family* takes *its* traditions very seriously," because the traditions are something shared by the group as a whole, but you'd say "My *family* sat in *their* usual seats at the dining room table," because in this case the family is thought of as individual members sitting in different seats.

colloquial

Colloquial language, like the language in the cartoon dialogue on the next page, is the kind of language that people use when they're talking, especially when they're having everyday conversations. It includes interjections, contractions, and slang. It also often includes statements and questions that don't really count as complete sentences by the usual rules of grammar.

Caution: Colloquial language isn't only used in speech—it does get used in writing, especially in the written dialogue in stories but also in advertisements, text messages, emails, and other kinds of writing where the writer wants to have a friendly, down-to-earth tone. (You may have noticed we're using contractions freely in this book, for instance.) But beware: the more formal the writing is, the less appropriate it is to use colloquial language in it. It's generally a good idea not to write colloquially in your papers for school, applications for jobs, apologies for breaking your neighbor's window with a baseball, and so on.

Emma and Jasmine add some colloquial flavor to lunch hour.

See also: contraction, interjection

comma splice

A comma splice consists of two independent clauses connected only by a comma ("Max looked out the window, he saw a herd of antelopes stampeding down the street"). Comma splices are usually considered a punctuation error, so you should try to avoid them in one of four ways:

1. Since independent clauses are capable of standing as sentences on their own, you can simply write the clauses as separate sentences ("Max looked out the window. He saw a herd of antelopes stampeding down the street").

2. Independent clauses can be joined by a comma and a coordinating conjunction ("Max looked out the window, and he saw a herd of antelopes stampeding down the street").

3. You can also join independent clauses with a semicolon ("Max looked out the window; he saw a herd of antelopes stampeding down the street").

4. Lastly, you can reword the sentence to make one of the clauses a subordinate clause ("When Max looked out the window, he saw a herd of antelopes stampeding down the street").

Which of these solutions you use depends on how closely connected the two clauses are in their meaning. Use method #1 when the clauses express fairly unrelated ideas. Use method #2 or #3 if you want to make it clear that the clauses have something to do with each other. Method #4 is helpful for expressing more directly what the relationship between the two clauses is.

See also: fused sentence, run-on sentence

common noun

A common noun—like *pebble, beauty, question,* or *sardines*—is a noun that refers to an ordinary object, idea, action, or living thing; it's the opposite of a proper noun, like *Zimbabwe, Alexander the Great,* or *Alice in Wonderland.* You'll notice that common nouns usually don't get capitalized—except, of course, when they come at the beginning of a sentence. Common nouns also are more likely than proper nouns to have plural forms or to be used with an article or an adjective.

See also: proper noun

comparative degree

A collie is shaggier than a dalmatian.

The comparative degree is a way of using an adjective or adverb to compare some thing (or action or quality) to something else. For example, in the sentence above, *shaggier* is the comparative degree of the adjective *shaggy*—it makes it clear that collies have more shagginess than dalmatians. For most short adjectives you form the comparative by adding *–er.* For instance, *sweet* becomes *sweeter.* But there are some special spelling rules:

● If the adjective ends in a single vowel and a single consonant, you usually double the consonant before adding *–er: sad* becomes *sadder.*

● If the adjective ends in *e,* you usually form the comparative by just adding *–r: wise* becomes *wiser.*

- If the adjective ends in y, you usually form the comparative by replacing the *y* with *–ier*: *happy* becomes *happier*.

For longer adjectives and most adverbs, you can form the comparative by simply adding *more* to the word: "Climbing up the cliff was *terrifying*, but climbing back down was even *more terrifying*."

- **Exception:** The adjectives *good* and *bad* have unusual comparative forms. Rather than "gooder" and "badder," the comparatives are *better* and *worse*. Likewise, the comparative of the adverb *well* is also *better*. The comparative of the adverb *badly* can be either *worse* or *more badly*.

- **Useful tip:** Not all adjectives and adverbs have a comparative degree form. Some, like the adjective *only* and the adverb *once*, can only be used in the positive degree.

See also: periphrastic, positive degree, superlative degree

complement

A complement is a word, phrase, or clause that helps complete your understanding of something that was mentioned earlier in the sentence by telling you what it is or what quality it has. There are several different kinds of complements, which are named based on what part of the sentence they add to your knowledge of.

Not every complement is also a compliment.

- For instance, in the cartoon dialogue on the previous page, the phrase "almost beautiful" helps describe the grammatical subject ("that sculpture"), so it's called a **subject complement**.

- In the sentence "Most people find me *fascinating,*" the word "fascinating" helps tell what quality the grammatical object ("me") has, so it's an **object complement**.

- In the sentence "I find it strange *that you don't want to give me $20,*" the clause "that you don't want to give me $20" helps tell who or what the adjective "strange" refers to, so it's an **adjective complement**.

- **Other examples:** "You seem *sad* today."

  "Do you consider split infinitives *acceptable*?"

  "I'm glad *I agreed to come along.*"

See also: predicate adjective, predicate nominative

complex preposition

Put the vase on top of the bookcase.

A complex preposition (sometimes called a "compound preposition") is a phrase, like "on top of" in the sentence above, that acts like a single preposition in the grammar of the sentence. Many complex prepositions consist of two prepositions used together, like "up to" or "out of." Others consist of one or more prepositions along with another part of speech, like "in place of" or "due to."

Other Examples: "We played football *in spite of* the blizzard."

  "Vladimir took the bus *over to* Whitneyville."

  "Carry the boxes *in through* the front door."

complex sentence

If I were you, I'd tie my shoelaces.

A complex sentence is a sentence that has at least one **subordinate clause** in addition to its **independent clause**. For instance, in the sentence above, the independent clause "I'd tie my shoelaces" is combined with the subordinate clause "If I were you" to make a single sentence.

- **Other examples:** "I won't stop pestering you *until you tell me the answer.*"

  "Could you walk the dog *when you get home*?"

  "*Although it sounds exciting*, I'd rather not jump off the roof *because I prefer not to break my neck.*"

- **Useful tip:** The subordinate clause in a complex sentence can come before or after the independent clause, or it can even be embedded inside the independent clause, like the relative clause "who play chess" in the sentence "People *who play chess* usually have very logical minds."

See also: compound-complex sentence, compound sentence, embedding, simple sentence

complex transitive verb

I consider myself an expert on vampires.

A complex transitive verb is a transitive verb that not only takes a **direct object** (like all transitive verbs) but also takes an **object complement**. For instance, the verb *consider* in the sentence above is a complex transitive verb because its direct object (*myself*) has a complement ("an expert on vampires") that provides extra information about it.

There are not many complex transitive verbs in English. The most commonly used ones are *appoint, call, consider, crown, deem, designate, elect, find, label, make, name, think, title,* and *vote.* You'll notice that when these verbs are used as complex transitive verbs, they generally have to do with one person (the grammatical subject) viewing another person or thing (the direct object) in a particular way or officially changing what that person or thing is.

- **Other examples:** "Do you *find* me pretty?"

  "The class *elected* me secretary."

  "She *titled* her book *Welding for Beginners.*"

- **Useful tip:** All of the Examples above are in the active voice. But any complex transitive verb can also be used in the passive voice, as in the sentence "My brother was named Student of the Month for six months in a row." In this case, the complement ("Student of the Month") tells more about who or what the grammatical subject ("my brother") is, so we'd call it a **subject complement** rather than an object complement.

compound

Something that's compound has two or more parts where there would ordinarily be just one. Grammatically, lots of different things can be compound—words (*greenhouse*), subjects ("*Snakes, lizards,* and *turtles* are all reptiles"), verbs ("The engine *sputtered* and *died*"), objects ("Jasmine collects *rocks* and *seashells*"), and even whole sentences ("*The test was hard,* but *I think I did well*").

See also: compound adjective, compound object, compound predicate, compound sentence, compound subject, compound tense, compound word

compound adjective

There's a many-legged creature in the bathtub.

A compound adjective, like *many-legged* in the sentence above, is made up of two or more words joined together with hyphens. Most compound adjectives aren't in the dictionary. Instead, they're put together on the spur of the moment by a writer or speaker when there's no single word that will work as well.

▪ **Other examples:** "I can jump over a *seven-foot* wall."

"Esmeralda is an *out-and-out* liar."

"Don't miss this *once-in-a-lifetime* opportunity."

▪ **Useful tip:** If you're trying to figure out whether a phrase that modifies a noun is a compound adjective or not—which will help you decide whether to use hyphens between its words or not—try asking yourself whether each of the individual words by itself refers to the noun. If they all do, you aren't dealing with a compound adjective, and you don't need a hyphen. But if one or more of the words in the phrase doesn't describe the noun, it's a compound adjective and should usually be hyphenated. For instance, you might be able to say that there's a "legged" creature in the bathtub, but the word *many* describes the number of legs, not the creature itself—so "many-legged" is a compound adjective, and it gets the hyphen.

compound-complex sentence

Though this is a great party, I'm tired, and I'm going home.

A compound-complex sentence is a sentence that has two or more **independent clauses** and at least one **subordinate clause**. In the example above, "I'm tired" and "I'm going home" are independent clauses joined with the conjunction *and*. By themselves they form a compound sentence, which becomes a compound-complex sentence once the subordinate clause "Though this is a great party" is added.

- **Other examples:** (subordinate clauses in italics):
  "The Norse were excellent sailors, and they reached the New World *long before Columbus did.*"

  "Millions of people already lived in the Americas *when the Norse arrived*, so the discovery of America must have happened much earlier than that."

- **Useful tip:** The subordinate clause of a compound-complex sentence doesn't necessarily have to come before or after the independent clauses—it can be embedded inside an independent clause, like the relative clause "that you say" in the sentence "I like you, but sometimes the things *that you say* make me really angry."

See also: complex sentence, compound sentence, embedding, simple sentence

compound object

My closet contains three pairs of old sneakers and a pile of dirty laundry.

A compound object consists of two or more noun phrases that are the objects of the same verb or preposition. For instance, in the sentence above, the object of the verb *contains* is a compound object, because it consists of the noun phrases "three pairs of old sneakers" and "a pile of dirty laundry."

Most of the time the noun phrases in a compound object are connected by the coordinate conjunction *and,* but if there are more than two noun phrases, you can use a comma in place of all the *and*s except the last one.

A compound object of a verb can be either a direct object or an indirect object.

- **Other examples:** "According to this recipe we need *a pineapple, two bananas,* and *fifteen coconuts.*" (compound direct object)

  "Mr. Zielinski gave *Emma* and *Vlad* different assignments." (compound indirect object)

  "We had to crawl through the opening on *hands* and *knees.*" (compound object of a preposition)

- **Useful tip:** Though almost all compound objects use *and* as a connector, it is possible to connect the phrases of a compound object by another coordinating conjunction, such as *but* ("Hawaii has *many native species of birds* but *very few mammals*").

See also: compound predicate, compound subject

compound predicate

We lit the fuse and ran for our lives.

A clause has a compound predicate if its grammatical subject is paired with two or more main verbs, as in the sentence above, where *we* is the subject of the verbs *lit* and *ran.* The verbs in a compound predicate may stand alone with no objects, or each may have its own direct or indirect object, or they may share an object.

- **Other examples:** "The musicians *smiled* and *bowed.*" (Neither verb has an object.)

  "I *remembered* my pen but *forgot* my notebook." (Both verbs have direct objects.)

  "She *asked* me a riddle and then *told* me the answer." (Both verbs have indirect and direct objects.)

  "This machine *peels, cores,* and *slices* the apples." (All three verbs share one direct object.)

- **Caution:** Since a compound predicate is defined by having two or more main verbs, the number of auxiliary verbs (like *can* or *must*) has nothing to do with it. The sentence "I *must have been thinking* of someone else" doesn't have a compound predicate, because it has only one main verb (*thinking*). But "I *have washed* and *folded* the laundry" does have a compound predicate, because it has two main verbs (*washed* and *folded*).

See also: compound object, compound sentence

compound preposition ^{See} complex preposition

compound sentence

A compound sentence is a sentence that has two or more **independent clauses** but no **subordinate clauses.** In the cartoon below, both independent clauses have the same subject (*I*), but in other compound sentences the clauses have different subjects.

I SENTENCE YOU TO FIVE YEARS FOR THE BURGLARY, AND I AM ADDING SIX MONTHS FOR THE DAMAGE TO MRS. CALLAHAN'S ROSES.

The defendant receives a compound sentence.

■ **Other examples:** "*You bring the peanut butter,* and *I'll bring the jelly.*"

"*I'm trying to write a poem,* but *it's hard to think of a rhyme for* crabapple."

■ **Useful tip:** The clauses of a compound sentence are most often connected by a comma and a coordinating conjunction such as *and* or *but*. But sometimes they're connected by just a semicolon ("They won; we lost"), a colon ("The rule is simple: for every action there's an equal and opposite reaction"), or a dash ("Everything's ready—off we go!"). If the sentence has several short clauses arranged as a list, it's not unusual for them to have just a comma between each two clauses except the last two: "*The rain stopped, the sun came out,* and *the pavement began to dry.*"

See also: complex sentence, compound-complex sentence, simple sentence

compound subject

Stripes and polka dots look strange together.

A grammatical subject is compound when it consists of two or more nouns (or noun phrases) that share the same verb, as *stripes* and *polka dots* do in the sentence above. Most of the time the nouns in a compound subject are connected by the coordinate conjunction *and*, but if there are more than two nouns, you can use a comma in place of all the *and*s except the last one. A compound subject connected with an *and* (or commas and an *and*) usually takes a plural verb.

- **Other examples:** "*Emma* and *I* are working on a chemistry project."

  "*Max* and *his cousin* are both left-handed."

  "*Two pennies, a dime,* and *a nickel* were all I found under the sofa cushions."

- **Useful tip:** Though almost all compound subjects use *and* as a connector, it is possible to connect the phrases of a compound subject in other ways, for instance by using a pair of correlative conjunctions like *either/or* or *neither/nor*: "Neither *ice hockey* nor *badminton* is played with a ball." When you construct a compound subject this way, the usual rule is that the verb should be singular if the last noun in the subject is singular, and it should be plural if the last noun in the subject is plural: "Neither *skates* nor *a bat* is used in soccer."

See also: compound object, correlative conjunction

compound tense

I am learning to dive.

A compound tense is a tense that not only tells whether the sentence has to do with the past, present, or future, but also involves information about **aspect**: whether the events described simply happen or whether they're finished or still going on at the point in time the sentence is talking about. It's the opposite of **simple tense**. For example, the present progressive sentence above is in a compound tense; it makes it clear that the act of learning to dive is still going on.

- **Other examples:** "It *had rained* all week."

  "I *have finished* my homework."

  "By this time tomorrow I *will be relaxing* on the beach."

- **Useful tip:** It's possible for a compound tense to involve more than one aspect at once, as in the past perfect progressive sentence "I *had been thinking deeply* for several minutes when I tripped on my shoelace and fell down."

See also: future perfect, future progressive, past perfect, past progressive, present perfect, present progressive

compound word

Nothing is quite as hunger-satisfying as octopus pie.

A compound word is made up of two or more shorter words used together as if they were a single word, like *backtalk.* The two words may be run together with no space, like *fruitcake* or *houseboat,* or they may be hyphenated or written as separate words, like *long-forgotten* or *cell phone.*

- **Other examples:** *headache, starfish, day-to-day, bald eagle, Los Angeles*

- **Useful tip:** If you're trying to decide whether to write a compound word as a single word or whether to leave a space or use a hyphen between its parts, try looking it up in a good dictionary. If the compound you're looking for isn't in the dictionary (for instance, if you can't find *octopuspie* or *hungersatisfying*), it's best to use a space between the parts if the compound word is acting as a noun and a hyphen if it's acting as an adjective: "Nothing is quite as *hunger-satisfying* as *octopus pie.*"

See also: compound adjective

concrete noun

Concrete nouns—like *chicken, hairdresser, island, snowstorm,* and *electron*—directly refer to objects, people, places, or events. Many proper nouns are also concrete nouns, since they refer to objects (*Empire State Building*), people (*Frederick Douglass*), places (*Antarctica*), or events (*Boston Tea Party*). Some proper nouns, though, are abstract rather than concrete (examples include *Islam* and *Impressionism*).

- **Useful tip:** Many readers find concrete nouns more interesting than abstract ones. To keep your writing lively, it's a good idea to use concrete nouns to illustrate your points. Even if you're writing about an abstract subject like honesty or justice, concrete examples will help your readers to understand your ideas. If you're writing about honesty, you might discuss a situation where somebody finds a *wallet* full of *cash* and *credit cards* lying in the *street*. If you're writing about justice, you might illustrate your points with the example of someone who is caught stealing someone else's *lunch* from a *school locker*.

See also: abstract noun, proper noun

conditional

If you want to make an omelet, you have to break some eggs.

The conditional is the form of sentence you use to discuss the results or effects of things that may or may not be true, as in the sentence above. A conditional sentence usually consists of two clauses:

1. a subordinate clause that describes the thing that may or may not be true ("If you want to make an omelet . . .")

2. an independent clause that describes something else that depends on whether the first thing is true ("you have to break some eggs").

Either of the two clauses can come first in the sentence. When the subordinate clause comes first, it's usually followed by a comma. However, no comma is needed when the independent clause comes first: "You have to break some eggs if you want to make an omelet."

In a conditional sentence about something that's a real possibility, the two clauses are both in the indicative mood ("If the tea *contains* arsenic, it *is* a bad idea to drink it"). In a sentence about something that is extremely unlikely or that you know isn't true, the subordinate clause is written with a **subjunctive conditional** verb ("If the tea *contained* arsenic . . .") and the independent clause is written with a subjunctive conditional **modal verb** (". . . it *would be* a bad idea to drink it").

■ **Other examples:** "*If today is Tuesday,* I have a cello lesson."

"We'll play basketball this afternoon *unless it rains.*"

"*If I knew the answer,* I might tell you."

■ **Useful tip:** The subjunctive conditional verb form that you use in the subordinate clause of a conditional sentence looks a lot like a past-tense verb, doesn't it? In fact, the subjunctive conditional verb used in present-tense sentences is identical to the past-tense verb, except for the forms of the verb *to be*—instead of "if *I was*," or "if *she was*," the subjunctive conditional form is "if *I were*," "if *she were*," etc.

See also: conditional conjunction, indicative

conditional conjunction

A conditional conjunction, such as *unless* in the sentence below, is used to introduce the subordinate clause of a conditional sentence. In some cases the conjunction takes the form of a phrase rather than a single word: "I'll give you half of my sandwich *provided that* you promise to stop pestering me."

Emma should have waited for the conditional conjunction.

- **Other examples:** *as long as, if, on the condition that, with the exception that*

- **Exception:** Not every conditional sentence has a conditional conjunction to introduce its subordinate clause. Conditional sentences can also be constructed starting with *had* or *were*, as in "*Had I known* you were there, I would have knocked before entering" or "*Were you to invite* me to the ball, I might consider accepting the invitation." These constructions are rare in everyday English—they're used more in formal speech and writing.

conjugate

To conjugate a verb is to list the various forms it takes in various tenses and aspects when it's paired with different kinds of subjects: singular or plural, first person or second person or third person. For instance, the verb *to be* gets conjugated as follows in the simple present tense:

	Singular	Plural
1st person	I *am*	we *are*
2nd person	you *are*	you *are*
3rd person	he/she/it *is*	they *are*

We could go on to construct similar tables showing the forms of *to be* in the simple past tense, or the past perfect, or the present progressive, or the future perfect progressive. Most of these tables would be rather unexciting, though, since the verb forms don't vary much in a lot of the tenses and aspects. Here, for example, is the conjugation for *to be* in the past perfect:

	Singular	Plural
1st person	I *had been*	we *had been*
2nd person	you *had been*	you *had been*
3rd person	he/she/it *had been*	they *had been*

Pretty boring, at least for English verbs! But if you study foreign languages like Spanish or German, you'll find that knowing how to conjugate verbs is very helpful. And in English, knowing how to conjugate a verb is useful when you're trying to identify finite verbs, which are a crucial part of every sentence—you can't have a complete sentence without a clause, and you can't have a clause without a finite verb.

See also: finite verb

conjunction

Either that wallpaper goes or I do!

Conjunctions, such as *and, if, although, unless*, and *nor*, are one of the **parts of speech**. They're used to join

- two words that belong to the same part of speech ("pepperoni *and* mushrooms")
- two phrases that play similar grammatical roles ("short on money *but* full of hope")
- two clauses ("*Either* that wallpaper goes *or* I do").

They can also connect a single word to a phrase or clause that acts as the same part of speech as that word does: "*alone* and *far from home*."

■ **Other examples:** "The horse ran <u>up *and* down</u> the hill." (joins a preposition to a preposition)

"<u>I laugh *whenever* someone tickles me.</u>" (joins a clause to a clause)

"I thought about <u>Rosalind *and* what I would say to her when we met.</u>" (joins a noun to a noun clause)

See also: conditional conjunction, conjunctive adverb, coordinating conjunction, correlative conjunction, subordinating conjunction

conjunctive adverb

Emma wanted to adopt the baby skunk that followed her home; however, her father vetoed the idea.

A conjunctive adverb, such as *therefore, besides,* or *however,* is an adverb that can help show what one clause has to do with the clause before it. In the example above, the conjunctive adverb *however* shows that the fact in the second clause ("her father vetoed the idea") overrules the fact in the first clause ("Emma wanted to adopt the baby skunk that followed her home").

Because it links grammatical parts of the same sort, a conjunctive adverb acts a lot like a conjunction. But unlike a conjunction, a conjunctive adverb usually can't be paired with a comma to join two clauses. Instead, it is usually paired with a semicolon ("It's too late for me to take you there; *besides,* I don't remember the way") or even a period ("Thanks, but I've already eaten. *Besides,* I'm pretty sure I'm allergic to octopus"). These punctuation marks signal more of a break between the clauses than a comma does.

■ **Useful tip:** If a conjunctive adverb comes in the middle of a clause instead of between clauses, it usually gets commas before it and after it ("Unicorns don't exist; what you saw, *therefore,* must not have been a unicorn").

■ **Other examples:** *also, furthermore, nevertheless, then, thus*

See also: comma splice

construction

In everyday English, a "construction" is something that has been put together from several parts. In grammar, a construction is a group of words put together to say something. Phrases are constructions. So are clauses and sentences—even when they're put together badly.

One reason for studying grammar is to learn which kinds of constructions are considered OK and which ones are considered to be mistakes. For example, sentences in which multiple negatives reinforce rather than contradict each other, like "I don't have no time to listen to your complaints," are common in many varieties of spoken English, but they're normally considered mistakes in writing. Sometimes a construction that is acceptable in one century comes to be seen as a mistake later on. For instance, a construction like "the *most unkindest*" was perfectly fine in the 1500s (Shakespeare used it in his play *Julius Caesar*), but any English teacher nowadays would mark it as a mistake if you used it in your own writing.

See also: double genitive, double negative, parallel construction, split infinitive, zero copula

content word

A content word (sometimes called a "lexical word") is a word like *sharp, anticipate, goggle,* or *far* that directly describes the people, things, actions, events, or qualities that a sentence is about. All nouns, verbs, and adjectives are content words, and so are most adverbs.

A lot of the meaning in a sentence comes from the meanings of its different content words—but the meaning of a sentence also comes from how the content words fit together with function words like *the* or *in,* as well as from the overall order of the words and the punctuation marks that go along with them—or from the speaker's tone of voice, if the sentence is spoken instead of written.

Most content words, unlike function words, can be inflected—that is, they can change form to express slightly different meanings (*sharp* might become *sharper* or *sharpest, anticipate* could become *anticipates* or *anticipated,* and so on).

See also: inflection, function word

continuous aspect See progressive aspect

contraction

When you run two words together as if they were one and you don't pronounce all the sounds of the words, you're using a contraction. Sometimes the contraction has a different vowel sound from the words being contracted. For instance, instead of saying "I do not like chicken," you might say "I *don't* like chicken." When you write a contraction, you leave out the letters that stand for the unpronounced sounds and put an apostrophe in their place.

- **Other examples:** *can + not = can't*
  they + have = they've
  we + will = we'll
  she + would = she'd
  I + am = I'm

- **Exception:** When you make a contraction out of *will* and *not*, it doesn't work the same way most other contractions do. You don't just replace some of the letters with an apostrophe, you also change the *i* to an *o*. So the contracted form is not "willn't" but "won't."

- **Useful tip:** Contractions are based on the way people talk every day. For everyday writing, it's OK to use contractions, but for assignments and other special occasions, such as book reports or essays, you might want to dress up your speech a little and avoid contractions.

coordinate clause

I'm no expert on knitting, but that doesn't look right to me.

When you use a comma and a coordinating conjunction (such as the *but* in the sentence above) to join two or more independent clauses, the clauses are called coordinate clauses.

- **Other examples:** "*The day was cloudy*, and *there was a cold wind*."
  "*The table is set, dinner is in the oven*, yet *none of the guests have arrived*."
  "*I have to go*, or *I'll be late for the game*."

- **Useful tip:** Coordinate clauses can also be joined with a semicolon instead of with a comma and a coordinating conjunction: "*Redwoods are* *the tallest trees in the world but not the largest; some giant sequoias are thicker and heavier."*

See also: compound sentence

coordinating conjunction

Like all **conjunctions**, a coordinating conjunction is a word that connects one part of a sentence to another. Coordinating conjunctions, such as *and, but, or, so,* or *yet,* are useful when the parts you're connecting have a similar grammatical form or purpose:

- A coordinating conjunction can connect one single word to another, like a noun to a noun ("bread *and* butter") or an adjective to an adjective ("tired *yet* happy").

- It can also connect larger parts of the sentence to other parts of the same kind, like a phrase to a phrase ("over the hill *or* around it"), a predicate to a predicate ("remembered my shoes *but* forgot my socks"), or a clause to a clause ("My glasses are broken, *so* I can't read the words").

- A coordinating conjunction is sometimes even used to link one sentence to another ("It's late. *And* I'm getting tired").

- **Caution:** Some people (including some teachers) feel that it's a bad idea to begin a sentence with a coordinating conjunction—especially *and* or *but.* It's definitely a bad idea to rely on these conjunctions too much as a way of keeping your reader moving from one sentence to another, because it's pretty boring to read a whole string of sentences all beginning with the same word.

See also: correlative conjunction, subordinating conjunction

coordination

Coordination is the relationship between different words, phrases, or clauses that play a similar grammatical role in a particular sentence.

Most of the time coordination is signaled by means of a **coordinating conjunction** (as in "*chickens* and *ducks*"), but coordination between clauses can also be signaled by a semicolon ("*It's dark; I can't see anything*"). Coordination of three or more parts is usually signaled by putting commas between them, often with a coordinating conjunction between the last two parts ("*words, phrases,* or *clauses*").

Coordinated adjectives and adverbs rarely have conjunctions between them when they directly modify another word ("a *tall, dark, handsome* stranger"), though they're still usually separated by commas.

It takes more than grammatical coordination to make a good juggler.

- **Other examples:** "*sang* and *danced*" (verbs in coordination)

  "walked *up* and *down* the stairs" (prepositions in coordination)

  "*out of the frying pan* and *into the fire*" (prepositional phrases in coordination)

  "*madly, passionately, violently* in love" (adverbs in coordination)

See also: coordinating conjunction

correlative conjunction

Most likely either a large seagull or a small velociraptor left those tracks.

Correlative conjunctions, like coordinating conjunctions, connect words, phrases, or clauses that play the same role in the grammar of the sentence. Unlike coordinating conjunctions, though, correlative conjunctions come in pairs, such as *either/or* or *both/and*. In the example above, the conjunctions are connecting two noun phrases ("a large seagull"; "a small velociraptor"), but correlative conjunctions can connect all the same kinds of sentence parts that coordinating conjunctions do.

When you use correlative conjunctions to link two sentence parts, one conjunction from the pair goes in front of the first part and the other conjunction goes in front of the second part. This is different from coordinating conjunctions, which usually only go between the parts that you're linking.

- **Other examples:** "You can choose *either* <u>archery</u> *or* <u>ballet</u> for your afternoon activity." (connecting two nouns)

  "Playing the kazoo is *neither* <u>difficult</u> *nor* <u>dangerous</u>." (connecting two adjectives)

  "It's really nice of you to both <u>cook the dinner</u> *and* <u>wash the dishes</u>." (connecting two bare infinitive phrases)

See also: coordinating conjunction, subordinating conjunction

count noun

A noun is a count noun if it's used to refer to a thing or things that can be either singular or plural. For instance, you could speak of "a bicycle" or "two bicycles" or "95 million bicycles," so *bicycle* is a count noun in all of these phrases. However, you wouldn't ordinarily speak of "an electricity" or "two electricities" or "95 million electricities," so *electricity* is not a count noun. (In fact, a word like electricity is called a **noncount noun**.)

When a count noun is singular, it is usually used with a definite or indefinite article ("*the* bicycle"; "*a* bicycle"), with a demonstrative ("*this* bicycle"), or with some adjective that acts as a **determiner** ("*any* bicycle"; "*your* bicycle").

- **Other examples:** *attic, daughter, instant, pancake, weed*

- **Useful tip:** Many nouns can be either count nouns or noncount nouns depending on how you use them in a sentence. For example, *memory* is a noncount noun when you're talking about the idea of remembering or the overall ability to remember ("Human *memory* is not always reliable"), but it's a count noun if you're talking about a particular thing that's being remembered ("I have a distinct *memory* of getting lost in the supermarket when I was very young" or "She has happy *memories* of her trip to the mountains").

See also: noncount noun

dangling modifier

Crawling across the road, Vladimir saw a snapping turtle.

A modifier is said to be "dangling" if it's in a position where it appears to modify something other than what the speaker or writer meant it to modify. For instance, in the sentence above, the reader would tend to assume that the participial phrase "crawling across the road" refers to the subject (*Vladimir*) instead of the object (*snapping turtle*), because modifiers are usually placed close to the things they modify in the sentence. Because dangling modifiers are likely to be confusing, it's a good idea to try to avoid them by being careful about where you place your modifiers: "Vladimir saw a snapping turtle *crawling across the road.*"

- **Other examples:** *"Having eaten my homework,* I angrily yelled at my dog."

  "Being bright red and steaming, she decided the lobsters were cooked."

  "Lost and far from its home, the family offered shelter to the hungry kitten."

- **Useful tip:** Because so many dangling modifiers are participial phrases, they're sometimes called "dangling participles."

- **Useful tip:** Many dangling modifiers have nothing to modify in the sentence because the writer assumes the reader will understand the context. For instance, in the sentence *"Reaching the top of the hill,* the city lights looked beautiful," the writer probably assumes that readers would understand who it was that reached the top of the hill.

See also: absolute construction

declarative sentence

There is a jaguar on the branch just above your head.

A declarative sentence, such as the one above, is a sentence that makes a statement of some kind, as opposed to one that asks a question, tells someone to do something, or expresses a feeling. In writing, declarative sentences usually end with a period, though you can also use an exclamation point once in a while to emphasize a particular sentence.

- **Other examples:** "Mars is the fourth planet from the sun."

  "The inning ended when the third batter struck out."

  "Emma will present her rocketry project tomorrow."

- **Useful tip:** Though ordinary questions, requests, and expressions of feeling aren't declarative sentences, they can often be rephrased as declarative sentences by turning them into statements. For instance, the question "Why did you do that?" can be rephrased as "I don't understand why you did that." The request "Stop making that noise!" can be rephrased as "I'd like you to stop making that noise." And the exclamation "What a gorgeous sunset!" can be rephrased as "That sunset is really gorgeous."

See also: exclamatory sentence, indicative, imperative, interrogative sentence

definite article

Please hand me the blue mixing bowl.

There's only one definite article in English: the word *the*. It's used as a **determiner** before nouns that refer to specific people, places, objects, actions, or ideas. The thing the noun refers to may be specific for any of various reasons:

- because it's one of a kind ("*the* North Pole")
- because it has already been mentioned ("I tried to use *a* spoon to stir the batter, but *the* spoon bent.")
- because the modifiers attached to the noun make it clear which thing you're referring to ("Please hand me *the blue* mixing bowl").

- **Other examples:** "Which of us is *the better* swimmer?"

  "Many alligators live in *the* Everglades."

  "I dreamed I was in an empty room. The walls of *the* room were covered with pictures of clocks."

See also: article, indefinite article

degree

This is the softest mattress we have.

Adjectives (and adverbs) take different forms depending on what their purpose is:

- simply describing a particular quality

- comparing the quality of one thing with another

- naming one thing as having the most or least of that particular quality.

These different forms are called degrees. For instance, the adjective *soft* in the sentence "I prefer a *soft* mattress on my bed" is in the positive degree—it simply describes the mattress as having the quality of softness. The adjective *softer* in "Can you get me a *softer* mattress?" is in the comparative degree—it describes the softness of one mattress in comparison to another. The adjective *softest* in "This is the *softest* mattress we have" is in the superlative degree, because it describes the mattress as having the most softness of any of the mattresses.

> **Useful tip:** Many short adjectives (and some adverbs) can be changed from the positive degree to the comparative by adding *–er* or to the superlative by adding *–est*. But longer adjectives (and most adverbs) are changed to the comparative just by adding the word *more* before them ("a *more* important fact"), and they're changed to the superlative by adding the word *most* ("the *most* important fact").

See also: comparative degree, periphrastic, positive degree, superlative degree

demonstrative

What is that on your shirt?

A demonstrative, such as *this* or *that,* is a word that you use to indicate which thing or things you're referring to. Demonstratives are used in two ways:

- They can be used as a **determiner** to introduce a noun phrase, as in "*this* piece of partly chewed bubblegum" or "*that* little gnome statue in the garden."

- Or they can stand alone as pronouns, as in "*This* is an ostrich egg" or "What is *that* on your shirt?"

If you're referring to a single thing that's fairly close to where you are, use *this*: "*this* pebble in my hand." If you're referring to a thing that's fairly far away, use *that*: "*that* mountain on the horizon." If you're referring to multiple things, use *these* if they're nearby ("*these* pieces of paper") and *those* if they're far away ("*those* players on the field").

- **Useful tip:** Demonstratives can also be used to refer to abstract things such as ideas, systems, facts, or problems. Since abstract things are neither close nor far away, you use a different system to decide which demonstrative to use. Use *this* (or *these*) for things that you're <u>about to mention</u> ("The solution is *this*: you have to explain the situation to her and ask her to help"), and use *that* (or *those*) for things that have <u>already been mentioned</u> ("I'm too modest. *That is* my only flaw").

dependent clause   **See** subordinate clause

determiner

A determiner is a word that begins a noun phrase and helps to make it clear whether the thing you're talking about is specific or general, or whether it's near or far, or whether it belongs to someone in particular, or whether there's only one thing or several—or none.

Determiners can be definite articles ("*The* Fourth of July") or indefinite articles ("*an* older sister"), or they can be demonstrative adjectives ("*those* ham sandwiches"), possessive adjectives ("*his* sneakers"), or other kinds of adjectives that help answer the question "Which?" or "How many?"

- **Other examples:** "*no* free lunch"

  "*either* half of the apple"

  "*seventy* slithering eels"

- **Useful tip:** In some cases two or more words may act together as a determiner, as the phrase *a number of* does in the sentence "A number of people walked out of the theater halfway through."

See also: article, definite article, demonstrative, indefinite article, possessive

diminutive

A diminutive is an **affix** that you use to show that something is small or young or cute. For instance, the suffix *–let* can be tacked onto the noun *book* to make *booklet* (a little book), or onto *drop* to make *droplet* (a tiny drop), or onto *pig* to make *piglet* (a young pig). Most of the diminutives in English words are suffixes rather than prefixes, though we have borrowed a few diminutive prefixes from Latin and Greek, such as the *mini–* in *miniskirt* or the *micro–* in *microchip*.

The diminutive suffix *–y* or *–ie* is especially associated with the idea of cuteness or affection. Thus we often say *doggie, horsie,* or *dolly* when we want to emphasize how cute or adorable the thing we're talking about is.

For some pets the diminutive just doesn't seem appropriate.

- **Other examples:** *kitchen + –ette = kitchenette*
  statue + –ette = statuette
  duck + –ling = duckling

- **Useful tip:** In many cases, you may not be able to figure out the full meaning of a diminutive word, such as *chaplet* or *stripling*, just by removing the diminutive affix to see what word it's based on. And some words that look like they have diminutive affixes, such as *etiquette* or *ceiling*, aren't diminutive at all. But if you do see a diminutive affix on an unfamiliar word, it's likely that the word refers to something small, young, or cute. (Incidentally, a *chaplet* is a small wreath worn on the head; a *stripling* is an adolescent.)

direct discourse

Jasmine said, "I'll be a little late getting home."

Direct discourse—also called "direct quotation"—is language that presents somebody's speech or writing in his or her own words. When you're writing direct discourse, you ordinarily put quotation marks at the beginning and end of the person's words, to show that you're quoting directly.

For example, in the sentence above, the phrase "I'll be a little late getting home" is written in direct discourse, so it's surrounded by quotation marks. However, in a sentence like "Jasmine said that *she'd be a little late getting home,*" the phrase "she'd be a little late getting home" is not in direct discourse (what kind of person refers to herself as "she"?), so it doesn't need to be in quotation marks.

■ **Other examples:** *"Why are frogs falling from the sky?"'* I asked.
  "I have no idea," he replied.

See also: ellipsis, indirect discourse

direct object

Vladimir certainly likes marshmallows!

A direct object, such as the word *marshmallows* in the sentence above, is the noun or noun phrase standing for whoever or whatever is experiencing the action that the verb describes. (The "action" of the verb isn't always something physical—in this case the marshmallows are experiencing the "action" of being liked by Vladimir.)

The direct object, if there is one, usually comes after the verb or verb phrase. If the direct object is a personal pronoun, it's ordinarily an objective pronoun such as *me, us, you, her, him, it,* or *them.* If the object of the sentence is a pronoun standing for the same person or thing as the subject of the sentence, the direct object can be a reflexive pronoun such as *myself, ourselves, yourself, herself, himself, itself,* or *themselves.*

■ **Other examples:** "The princess kissed *the frog.*"

  "Do you own *a digital camera?*"

  "I have forgotten *the way to your house.*"

■ **Caution:** Not every verb has a direct object. In some sentences, such as "The cold rain fell," the predicate consists of just a verb by itself (*fell*). And sentences with linking verbs technically don't have direct objects— instead, they have subject complements, like the phrase "a swamp" in the sentence "The dirt road became *a swamp* after three weeks of rain."

■ **Useful tip:** Even though they don't count as verbs grammatically, infinitives and participles can also have direct objects, as in the sentence "He fell off the unicycle, bruising *his left elbow*."

See also: indirect object, subject complement, transitive verb

double genitive

A double genitive is a construction that uses both the word *of* and a possessive form (usually – *'s*) to show the relation between one thing and another. For example, the phrase "a cousin *of Max's*" is a double genitive. The relationship between Max and his cousin could be indicated with just the *of* ("a cousin *of Max*") or with just the – *'s* ("*Max's cousin*").

■ **Caution:** Some people consider double genitive constructions to be a mistake, since it's not really necessary to use two different grammatical techniques to show a relationship that could be shown with just one. But most people, including many good writers, do sometimes use double genitives, especially with people's names (like *Max's* in "a cousin *of Max's*") or possessive pronouns (like *mine* in "a friend *of mine*").

See also: genitive, periphrastic, possessive pronoun

double negative

A double negative (as in the phrase "*didn't* say *nothing*") is a construction that uses two **negatives** to express an idea that could be expressed with a single negative (as in "said *nothing*" or "*didn't* say anything"). Double negatives are common and correct in many languages and are used in some varieties of spoken English. In fact, they were once considered OK by all speakers of English, but they're now usually regarded as a grammatical error in writing.

■ **Other examples:** "There *won't* be *no* school today."

"*Isn't* there *nothing* I can do to change your mind?"

"*Nobody can't* tell me what to do."

■ **Caution:** Not all sentences with two negatives in them are incorrect. Sometimes a sentence will actually need both negatives to make its point, as in "You *shouldn't* stand around and do *nothing* when you see somebody being bullied." And the rule against double negatives doesn't apply when the negatives fall in different clauses, as in "I *don't* like okra, and I *don't* care who knows it."

E

ellipsis

An ellipsis (the plural is *ellipses*) is a punctuation mark that looks like three periods in a row (. . .), which you use to show where you've left words out of a passage you're quoting. Ellipses are useful when the passage you're quoting is fairly long and includes extra information that you don't want to include. For instance, suppose you're writing about what bats eat, and you're quoting a book that says

> *Bats have a varied diet about which very little was known until relatively recently, but they mostly eat moths, mosquitoes, gnats, and night-flying beetles such as fireflies.*

In quoting this passage, you might choose to write it as

> *"Bats . . . mostly eat moths, mosquitoes, gnats, and . . . beetles such as fireflies."*

(You'd probably also want to tell the reader where the quoted passage comes from, especially if you're writing a paper for school. Ask your teacher for more information on how to do this.)

■ **Useful tip:** Many writers also use the ellipsis to represent a pause in someone's speech (as in "I don't know . . . perhaps I'll try a bowl of your octopus chili after all") or to show that a thought has not been fully expressed (as in "Well, if you're sure it's a good idea . . .").

See also: direct discourse

elliptical construction

I came in first, Vladimir second, and Max third.

An elliptical construction is a grammatical construction that leaves out some words that the grammar of the sentence would normally require. Elliptical constructions are common in everyday speech and are usually acceptable in writing when it's obvious which words have been left out.

For instance, in the sentence above, we can guess that Vladimir and Max are meant to be the subjects of clauses of their own, with the phrasal verb "came in" being left out because it's already appeared in the first clause.

- **Other examples:** "If [it is] possible, call me when you get there."

  "Where are you going?" "[I am going to] Tulsa."

  "I enjoy basketball more than [I enjoy] golf."

- **Caution:** Elliptical constructions can cause confusion when the reader or listener doesn't know for sure which words have been left out. Does "I like Emma more than you" mean "I like Emma more than *you like Emma*" or "I like Emma more than *I like you*"? It could make a big difference!

embedding

Be careful with that antique Chinese vase!

In everyday English, to "embed" something is to place it firmly into a surrounding mass (as when a post is embedded in concrete). In grammar, embedding is the process of placing one grammatical unit within another, larger unit. For instance, in the sentence above, the noun phrase "that antique Chinese vase" is embedded in the prepositional phrase "with that antique Chinese vase."

Many different kinds of phrases and clauses can be found embedded in other kinds of phrases or clauses. In fact, often one phrase or clause will be embedded in another, which is embedded in yet another, and so on.

- **Other examples:** "to forget *to call home*" (an infinitive phrase within another infinitive phrase)

  "having been to *Philadelphia*" (a prepositional phrase within a participial phrase)

  "the man *who won* <u>the dancing competition</u>" (a noun phrase embedded within a subordinate clause embedded within a noun phrase)

- **Useful tip:** The role a particular grammatical unit plays in a sentence depends on the overall unit, not on the grammatical role played by its embedded parts. For instance, the noun phrase "the sculpture that was made by gluing together thousands of toothpicks" has *sculpture* as its main noun. The noun is modified by an adjectival clause ("that was made by gluing together thousands of toothpicks"), which contains a gerund phrase ("gluing together thousands of toothpicks"), which contains a noun phrase ("thousands of toothpicks"), which contains a prepositional phrase ("of toothpicks"), which contains a noun (*toothpicks*). *Toothpicks* is obviously plural. But since the entire noun phrase is based on the singular noun *sculpture,* the noun phrase as a whole is singular and takes a singular verb—that is, you'd say "The sculpture that was made by gluing together thousands of toothpicks is very impressive," not "The sculpture that was made by gluing together thousands of toothpicks are very impressive."

See also: agreement

emphatic

An emphatic construction is one that uses a form of *do* as an auxiliary verb to emphasize a point. If you just say "Vlad knows how to juggle," you're simply making a statement. But if you say "Vlad *does* know how to juggle," you're drawing attention to the point you're making.

You might use the emphatic construction to reply to someone who doubts Vlad's juggling abilities ("I heard that Vlad can't juggle"), or to direct attention away from some other activity that Vlad isn't much good at ("Vlad isn't much of a sword-swallower, is he?"), or for some other purpose.

OH, I **DO** LOVE THE PRETTY FLOWERS! AND I **DO** LOVE THE PRETTY TREES! AND I **DO** LOVE THE PRETTY BIRDS!

Jasmine *does* get a bit emphatic sometimes.

■ **Other examples:** "I *did* hope you'd remember the sandwiches."

"We *do* need to hurry, or we'll be late."

"Strange as it sounds, some mammals *do* lay eggs."

exclamatory interrogation

Who cares what the neighbors think!

An exclamatory interrogation is a sentence that's phrased as a question but acts as a kind of exclamation, as in the example above. In speech, it's usually obvious from the speaker's tone of voice whether a sentence is an exclamation or a question. In writing, an exclamatory interrogation is often written with an exclamation point instead of a question mark.

- **Other examples:** "Would you look at that!"

   "Am I glad to see you!"

   "Isn't that the truth!"

See also: exclamatory sentence, interrogative sentence

exclamatory sentence

What an unusual hat!

An exclamatory sentence, such as "What an unusual hat!" or "To think that we lost the basketball game by just one point!" expresses strong feeling rather than stating a fact. As expressions of feeling, they serve a purpose similar to **interjections**, and like interjections they're usually punctuated with an exclamation mark. Often exclamatory sentences aren't even complete sentences at all—they can be just phrases or subordinate clauses with no independent clause, as in "What a rude person!" or "If only we had arrived a few minutes earlier!"

- **Other examples:** "As if you didn't already know!"

   "How strange!"

   "Thanks a million!"

See also: declarative sentence, exclamatory interrogation, interrogative sentence

F

factitive verb   **See** complex transitive verb

feminine

The feminine is a grammatical **gender**. Unlike in some languages where every noun has grammatical gender, the feminine in English appears in a limited number of grammatical forms:

- the subjective personal pronoun *she*
- the objective personal pronoun *her*
- the reflexive personal pronoun *herself*
- the possessive pronoun *hers*
- the possessive adjective *her.*

These words are mainly used in referring to girls and women, though they are also applied to female animals, to ships, and sometimes to nations or other large organizations that people feel loyalty to.

In addition to these feminine words, there are also a few nouns in English that have both masculine and feminine forms, like *Latino* and *Latina* or *prince* and *princess.* But many of the traditional feminine forms, such as *authoress* or *mayoress,* are not used much anymore and are often considered insulting. Instead, the traditionally masculine forms (like *author* or *mayor*) are used for both men and women.

See also: masculine, neuter

finite verb

Jasmine has been advancing very quickly in math.

A finite verb is a verb that takes a particular form (that is, it gets **in-flected**) to show the number and person of the subject and to show the tense of the verb. Every complete clause contains a finite verb in addition to any infinitives or participles that may also play a role in the verb phrase. In the example sentence above, for instance, the finite verb is the auxiliary *has*—the other words in the verb phrase are a past participle (*been*) and a present participle (*advancing*).

- **Other examples:** "Max *stubbed* his toe."

  "I *have* been thinking of moving to Antarctica."

  "To exercise daily *takes* a lot of willpower."

- **Exception:** Many auxiliary verbs only take a few different forms when they act as finite verbs—*can*, for instance, doesn't change based on the number or person of the subject ("we *can*," "you *can*," "she *can*," "they *can*," etc.)—the only way it's inflected is that it changes to *could* in the past tense. And *must* never changes at all, even to show tense. But auxiliaries like these can still count as finite verbs, and the words that follow them in a verb phrase will be in infinitive or participle form.

- **Useful tip:** It is possible for a clause to contain more than one finite verb, if it has a compound predicate: "The deer *jumped* across the brook and *vanished* into the trees."

See also: infinitive, participle, verb phrase

first person

The first person is the category of grammatical forms that you use when you're referring to yourself—either yourself alone or yourself and other people. The only parts of speech that have first-person forms are pronouns, possessive adjectives, and verbs.

- The first-person pronouns are *I, me, myself,* and *mine* (used when you're referring only to yourself) and *we, us, ourselves,* and *ours* (used when you're referring to yourself and other people).

- The first-person possessive adjectives are *my* and *our.*

- For most verbs, the first-person singular and plural forms are the same as the second-person singular and plural and the third-person plural: "I *yell,*" "we *yell,*" "you *yell,*" and "they *yell,*" for instance. (For the verb *be,* see the chart at the entry for **conjugate**.)

- **Caution:** First-person plural pronouns always include the speaker or writer—but they may or may not include the readers or listeners. This can cause confusion. If you think your reader or listener won't know what you mean by saying "Emma told me *we've* been nominated for class president," you might want to rephrase it to "Emma told me *she and I* have been nominated for class president" or "Emma told me *you and I* have been nominated for class president."

See also: agreement, second person, third person

fragment

A fragment (or "sentence fragment") is a string of words that begins with a capital letter and ends with a period but isn't a complete sentence, such as "Hopping up and down on one foot." Most of the time what makes something a fragment rather than a sentence is the fact that it doesn't have an independent clause. Fragments are usually considered to be errors, but fortunately they're usually easy to fix in one of three ways:

1. You can connect the fragment to the sentence before it, turning "I saw Vladimir. Hopping up and down on one foot." to "I saw Vladimir hopping up and down on one foot."

2. You can connect the fragment to the sentence after it, turning "Hopping up and down on one foot. Vladimir shouted in pain." to "Hopping up and down on one foot, Vladimir shouted in pain."

3. You can revise the fragment itself so that it includes an independent clause, turning "Hopping up and down on one foot." to "Vladimir hopped up and down on one foot."

Vlad has a fragmentary understanding of history.

Other examples: "Unless I hear from you before then."

"Having lost my way in the dark woods."

"Reaching under the car seat to search for any nickels, dimes, or quarters that might have slid under there over the course of the three years since we last got around to cleaning the car thoroughly."

See also: elliptical construction

function word

To tell the truth, I feel slightly scared.

A function word is a word whose main purpose is to show the relationships between the various things, people, ideas, or actions referred to in a sentence, rather than to describe or name those things, people, ideas, or actions. Function words can be articles, auxiliary verbs, conjunctions, demonstratives, negatives such as *no* or *not,* prepositions, or pronouns.

■ **Other examples:** "*After the* sun set, *the* woods were nearly—*but not* completely—silent."

"*That* little rustling noise *must have been* made *by a* squirrel or *a* mouse."

"*To* tell *the* truth, *I* feel slightly scared."

See also: content word

fused sentence

A fused sentence, like "It's a bad idea to swallow gravel don't do it!" is a construction in which two or more sentences are written as if they were one sentence, with no punctuation or conjunctions to join them together. Fused sentences are definitely considered to be errors, but the good news is that they're easy to fix, in one of three ways:

1. You can simply rewrite them as separate sentences. ("It's a bad idea to swallow gravel. Don't do it!")

2. If the ideas in the fused sentence are closely related to each other and if you think that their relationship will be obvious to any reader, you can use a semicolon to divide two independent clauses. ("It's a bad idea to swallow gravel; don't do it!")

3. If you want to make it perfectly clear what the ideas in the fused sentence have to do with other, you can use a comma and a conjunction to connect the parts. ("It's a bad idea to swallow gravel, *so* don't do it!")

■ **Other examples:** "Today is Tuesday tomorrow will be Wednesday."

"I told him if he didn't help me I wouldn't help him he said he didn't care."

"What's this is it a sea-urchin shell?"

See also: comma splice, run-on sentence

future perfect

In five minutes Max will have eaten ten pancakes!

The future perfect is a verb form—like the verb phrase "will have eaten" in the sentence above—that combines the **future tense** with the **perfect aspect**. You use the future perfect when you want to describe a time when some event or action will have happened or will have been completed.

The future perfect consists of the auxiliary verb *will* (which occurs in ordinary future-tense verbs) and the auxiliary verb *have* (which occurs in ordinary perfect-aspect verbs) along with the past participle of the main verb—the verb that describes the event or action.

■ **Other examples:** "In December I *will have lived* here for twelve years."

"He *won't have reached* the end of the chapter by the time the bus arrives."

"*Will* you *have finished* your homework by then?"

■ **Useful tip:** It's possible to construct more complex future perfect verb forms by combining the *will have* with a progressive ("If the candidate goes on speaking for one more minute she *will have been talking* for over two hours") or a passive construction ("All the cake *will have been eaten* before we get there").

See also: compound tense

future progressive

In a few more minutes Max will be feeling sick to his stomach.

The future progressive is a form of the verb, like the verb phrase "will be feeling" in the sentence above, that combines the **future tense** with the **progressive aspect.** You use the future progressive when you want to describe a future time when some event or action will be occurring.

The future progressive consists of the auxiliary verb *will* (which occurs in ordinary future-tense verbs) and the auxiliary verb *be* (which occurs in ordinary perfect-aspect verbs) along with the present participle of the main verb—the verb that describes the event or action.

- **Other examples:** "We *will be going* to the Ozarks this summer."

  "The forecast says it *will* still *be raining* tonight."

  "I*'ll be waiting* for you by the back door."

See also: compound tense

future tense

Jasmine will slip on the banana peel.

The future tense (sometimes called the "future time") is the verb form that you use to discuss events or actions that haven't happened yet. In English, you ordinarily put verbs into the future tense by adding the auxiliary verb *will* to the verb phrase. So, for example, the present-tense *slips* in "Jasmine *slips* on the banana peel" becomes the future-tense *will slip* in "Jasmine *will slip* on the banana peel." (Notice that when you add the *will*, the *slips* changes to the bare infinitive *slip*. This is because only the first verb in a verb phrase can be a **finite verb**—the rest will be infinitives or participles.)

- **Other examples:** "I *will pay* you back tomorrow."

  "The new president *will be inaugurated* in January."

  "On Saturday it *will be* six months since I moved to Whitneyville."

- **Useful tip:** In old-fashioned and formal English, you may occasionally see the future tense indicated by *shall* instead of *will*. The traditional rule is that when you use *will* with a first-person subject like *I* or *we*, it expresses your willingness to do the action the verb refers to ("I *will* tell you the answer"), and when you use *shall* with a first-person subject it expresses a simple prediction about the future ("I *shall* be thirteen in April"). With a second- or third-person subject, it's the other way around: *will* expresses your prediction about the future ("You *will* get rained on if you go outside"), and *shall* expresses your decision to make or allow the action or event to happen ("You *shall* not behave in that manner!"). But almost nobody follows this rule any more—almost everybody uses *will*, and the people who don't use *will* use a form of *be* along with the verb phrase "going to" (often shortened to *gonna* in speech) to express the future tense, as in "*I am going to* be thirteen in April."

See also: future perfect, future progressive, past tense, present tense

G

gender

In everyday life, gender has to do with whether you see yourself as being male or female, and how that affects your behavior. In grammar, words are said to have gender if they're divided into categories such as **masculine**, **feminine**, and **neuter**. In some languages, every noun is given a gender, and adjectives and articles take different forms to match. In French, for example, *porte* ("door") is feminine, so it gets paired with the feminine article *la* ("the") instead of the masculine *le* (also "the"). In German, *Apfel* ("apple") is masculine, so any adjectives that modify it get masculine endings rather than feminine ones—you'd say "*ein grosser* Apfel" ("a large apple") rather than "*eine grosse* Apfel." But in English, gender is much simpler: grammatical gender exists mostly in personal pronouns—when you're discussing a man or boy (or a male animal) you use masculine pronouns like *he* or *him*, and when you're discussing a woman or girl (or a female animal) you use feminine pronouns like *she* or *her*.

See also: number, person

genitive

The genitive is a **case** that shows that one noun is modifying another. There are two main ways you can use the genitive in English: either by putting the noun that's acting as a modifier first and adding *'s* to it, or by putting the modifier second as part of a prepositional phrase starting with *of*. You can also make pronouns genitive by using their possessive forms, such as *her, its,* or *their.*

The genitive serves any of several purposes:

- It can show that something belongs to someone ("That is *Emma's* bookbag").

- It can show that something is part of something else ("The center *of the earth* is extremely hot").

- It can show that something or someone is in a particular relationship to something or someone else ("*Max's* cousins refuse to eat anything but macaroni and cheese").

- It can show that something or someone has a particular quality ("Diamonds are known for *their* hardness and brilliance").

- It can describe something as existing in a particular amount or to a particular degree ("Please give me *three weeks'* notice before your visit").

- It can describe someone or something as doing something ("*her* sharpening of the pencil") or as being the one something is done to ("the discovery *of electricity*").

See also: double genitive, periphrastic, possessive, possessive pronoun

gerund

Don't you enjoy trying new foods?

A gerund, such as the word *trying* in the sentence above, looks like a verb, but it doesn't act like one. It is actually a **verbal** that acts as a noun. Gerunds are made from the present participle form of the verbs they're derived from, so they all end in *–ing*.

- **Other examples:** "*Walking* is an easy form of exercise."

  "I heard a *rustling* in the dry leaves behind me."

  "Jasmine apologized for *forgetting* my birthday."

- **Useful tip:** Not every present participle that appears in a sentence is a gerund! The present participle often appears in progressive-aspect verb phrases ("I have been *thinking* about joining the circus") and as an adjective, either by itself ("I heard a *rustling* sound in the dry leaves") or as part of a participial phrase ("The chipmunk, *rustling* in the dry leaves behind my back, startled me"). A present participle is only called a gerund if it's being used as a noun—that is, if it's a grammatical subject or if it's the object of a verb or preposition.

- **Useful tip:** Because a gerund isn't a real verb, it can't have a real grammatical subject. If you mention who's doing the action just before the gerund, you don't use the subjective case (that is, you don't say "*He* shivering made it hard to tie his shoes"). Instead, you use the possessive as you would with any other noun ("*His* shivering made it hard to tie his shoes").

See also: infinitive

habitual aspect

The habitual aspect in English mostly exists in verb phrases beginning with "used to," as in the dialogue below. This aspect of the verb is useful when you want to make it clear that something happened more than just once or twice or that something was a particular way for a long time. The name "habitual" may help you to remember its meaning, since habitual actions are habits—things you do over and over. But it's important to understand that the habitual aspect can be used for any kind of repeating or long-lasting event, even if it's not what would ordinarily be called a habit.

Judging by his grammar, he's a habitual liar.

- **Other examples:** "Myanmar *used to be called* Burma."

  "I *used to think* cauliflower tasted horrible."

  "I *used to walk* to school when I lived in Santa Rosa."

- **Caution:** Once upon a time, the English language had a present-tense form of the habitual "used to" too, not just a past-tense form. People used to say "I *use to drink* hot tea with my breakfast." But nowadays we ordinarily just use the simple present tense to express the same idea ("I *drink* hot tea with my breakfast"). If you see a sentence where someone has written "I *use to drink* hot tea with my breakfast," most likely the writer made a mistake and really meant the past-tense "used to." This mistake is common because when we say "used to," we often don't pronounce the "d" sound clearly—it gets swallowed up by the "t" sound.

Useful tip: The habitual aspect can also be expressed by the auxiliary verb *would* or *will*, as in the sentence "When I was younger I *would often ask* my grandfather to tell me stories." This construction almost always is used along with phrases or clauses that help to indicate the time in question, such as "In those days..." or "When I was a child...."

head

One of the best ways to cook eggs is by poaching them.

In everyday English, you're at the "head" of a line if you're first in the line, but in grammar, the head of a phrase isn't necessarily the first word in the phrase. Instead, the head of a phrase is the word that the phrase is built up around, such as the word *one* in the noun phrase "*one* of the best ways to cook eggs." All the other words in the phrase are just there to modify the head of the phrase. When a noun phrase is acting as the subject of a clause, you look at whether the head of the noun phrase is singular or plural to decide whether the verb should be singular or plural.

Verb phrases have heads too. The head of a verb phrase is the main verb—which may (or may not) have a string of auxiliary verbs and adverbs attached to it, as the word *regretted* does in the phrase "have always deeply *regretted*."

Other examples: "the lovely old Chinese *vase* on the bookcase"

"not having been *chosen*"

"the first full *day* of summer vacation"

See also: agreement, determiner, main verb

helping verb   See auxiliary verb

hierarchy of adjectives

Just look at that lovely new silver Italian mountain bike!

When you use a string of two or more adjectives to directly modify a noun, certain kinds of adjectives usually come before certain other kinds of adjectives, based on what kind of information they give about the noun they modify. The system for putting adjectives in their proper order is sometimes called the "hierarchy of adjectives."

The rule for this system may look complicated, but people who grew up speaking English already know them without having to think about it every time they string adjectives together. There is some flexibility in the rules, especially for different emphasis, but the usual order is as follows:

1. determiners, such as the articles *a* or *the,* the demonstratives *this* or *that,* the possessives *my* or *your,* or adjectives that tell how much (*some, all, no, many, most*)

2. adjectives that give a judgment about what something is like (*lovely, terrible*)

3. adjectives that tell how large something is (*huge, little*)

4. adjectives that tell what shape something is (*flat, slender*)

5. adjectives that tell how old something is (*new, ancient*)

6. adjectives that tell what color something is (*silver, many-colored, purple*)

7. adjectives that tell what something is made of (*wooden, fiberglass*)

8. capitalized adjectives (*Italian, Native American*)

9. adjectives or participles that tell the purpose of something ("*congratulatory* remarks," "*fishing* rod")

10. nouns that act as attributive adjectives ("*sand* painting" "*mountain* bike," "*ski* jacket").

■ **Other examples:** "a many-colored Native American sand painting"

"many slender gray fiberglass fishing rods"

"my purple ski jacket"

historical present

So I'm trying to get my kite down from the tree, and I've got this long stick, but what I don't realize is . . . .

If you're telling a story about something that happened in the past but you use the present tense to describe what happened, you're using the historical present. We commonly use the historical present in everyday speech when we want to tell about our recent experiences, as in the example above.

It's also traditional to use the historical present in speech or writing when you're retelling the plot of a book or movie ("The main character, Ethelbert, is a peasant in medieval England who wants to become a knight . . ."). For most other purposes you should use the past tense when you're discussing events that took place in the past.

idiom

An idiom, such as "way out of line" or "got her goat," is a phrase or other construction whose meaning isn't obvious to people who have never heard it before, even if they know all the words in the idiom and understand all the rules of English grammar. We use idioms all the time in speech, and they're common in informal writing, but in formal writing it's a good idea to avoid idioms as much as possible.

Using idioms, Emma and Vlad get down to brass tacks.

■ **Other examples:** "Time is *of the essence.*" ("Time is *extremely important*")

"You don't have to *beat around the bush.*" ("You don't have to *avoid talking openly about what's on your mind.*")

"I was *on cloud nine.*" ("I was *very, very happy.*")

■ **Useful tip:** Many children's and student dictionaries don't define idioms at all, or they include only a few of the most common idioms. Good adult dictionaries usually do include idioms, often listing them at the end of the entry that defines the first important word in the idiom. For instance, you might look for "at the drop of a hat" at the entry for *drop*, and "on the spur of the moment" at *spur*.

imperative

The imperative is one of the grammatical **moods** in English; it's the form of verb you use when you're directly telling somebody what to do. It isn't necessarily rude or bossy—you can use the imperative for making polite requests as well as for giving orders. The person being spoken to is the grammatical subject of the sentence, but quite often the person is not named in the sentence and the subject of the verb is not stated. Whether you address the person by name or not, the imperative form of the verb is always the same as if the grammatical subject were the word *you*.

- **Other examples:** "Come over here, Emma!"

  "Please take a seat."

  "Give me one reason why I shouldn't do it!"

- **Useful tip:** Traditionally sentences in the imperative mood were punctuated with an exclamation point. If the sentence is more of a request than an order, it's OK to use a period instead. An imperative sentence is never a question, so don't use a question mark.

imperfect aspect   See progressive aspect

indefinite adjective

Few rodeo riders are also ballet dancers.

Most of the words that can act as indefinite pronouns can also act as **determiners** at the beginning of noun phrases. When they're used this way—as *few* is in the sentence above—these words are known as indefinite adjectives.

- **Other examples:** "*Either* path will take us to the lake."

  "May I have *some* water?"

  "*Each* character in the game has a different set of powers."

- **Useful tip:** Some indefinite pronouns, such as *anything, everyone*, and *none*, can't be used as indefinite adjectives. And some indefinite adjectives, such as *many*, can be used either as determiners ("*Many* people find your sense of humor irritating") or as ordinary adjectives ("Your sense of humor is one of the *many* things I find irritating about you").

See also: indefinite pronoun

indefinite article

Can you lend me a pencil?

The indefinite articles *a* and *an* are used as **determiners** at the beginning of noun phrases. You use them when you're referring to one of several possible people, places, objects, actions, or ideas. For instance, in the sentence above, the indefinite article *a* makes it clear that you don't care *which* pencil you borrow—all that matters is that it can write. After you've used an indefinite article in mentioning somebody or something once, you usually switch to the definite article if you mention that same person or thing again: "*The* pencil needs sharpening."

- **Other examples:** "I would like *an* egg salad sandwich."

  "I have *a* neighbor who is *a* veteran."

  "*An* extremely large tree blew down in the park."

- **Useful tip:** You decide between *a* and *an* based on whether the word following it begins with a consonant or with a vowel—but this rule is based on the word's pronunciation, not on its spelling. If the word begins with a vowel sound, you use *an* regardless of how it's spelled—for example, you say "*an honest* person," not "*a honest* person."

See also: article, definite article

indefinite pronoun

I tried one door after another, but each was locked.

Like other types of pronouns, indefinite pronouns—such as *each, everyone, nothing,* and *some*—stand for nouns in the grammar of a sentence. You use indefinite pronouns when the people, places, objects, or ideas you're discussing are important not on their own, as individual items, but as belonging to a particular group. For instance, in the sentence above, *each* is an indefinite pronoun that treats the individual doors as members of a larger group of doors—the ones you're trying to open.

- **Other examples:** "*All* are invited."

  "Most insects have at least two wings, and *many* have four."

  "I've tried *everything* to get Jasmine's attention."

- **Useful tip:** You'll notice that most of the indefinite pronouns provide general information about *how many* or *how much* of something you're talking about.

See also: indefinite adjective, personal pronoun

independent clause

Suddenly I heard a strange hissing sound.

An independent clause is a **clause**—like the one above—that can stand alone as a sentence. Every complete sentence has at least one independent clause, and some sentences have two or more, usually connected with coordinating conjunctions such as *and* or *but*.

■ **Other examples:** "Although they can't fly, *penguins are excellent swimmers.*"

"*The Great Chicago Fire happened in 1871.*"

"*In soccer you can kick the ball or hit it with your head,* but *only goalies are allowed to touch it with their hands.*"

■ **Useful tip:** Unlike subordinate clauses, which always take the same form regardless of whether the sentences they appear in are declarative, imperative, or interrogative, independent clauses take different forms depending on the kind of sentence they appear in. In declarative sentences they're worded as statements ("If you really want to help, *I can think of some things you could do*"); in imperative sentences they're worded as requests or orders ("If you really want to help, *grab the other end of this board!*"); and in interrogative sentences they're worded as questions ("If you really want to help, *why are you standing around with your hands in your pockets?*").

See also: coordinating conjunction, main clause, subordinate clause

independent possessive   See possessive pronoun

indicative

That is some hot chili!!!

The indicative is the most common of the grammatical **moods** in English; it's the verb form you use when you're making a statement (as in the example above) or asking a question about the way things are or were or will be, as opposed to the way they could be or should be. Just like with the other moods, if you're trying to decide whether a sentence is in the indicative, you look at its verb forms. Only indicative verbs take different forms to show number and person—verbs in other moods are always the same regardless of whether their subject is singular or plural or in the first, second, or third person.

- **Other examples:** "How *did* you *get* here?"

  "Remembering those happy days *brings* tears to my eyes."

  "Unless I *hear* from you first, I'*ll plan* on meeting you at the hockey rink this afternoon."

- **Useful tip:** Though the indicative mood is mostly for discussing whether particular things did happen or are going to happen, you can also use the indicative mood in conditional sentences when the events you're talking about are still uncertain but have a pretty good chance of happening. For instance, if Emma is a pretty good athlete, you might say "She *will go* on to the state championships if she *beats* the other runners at tomorrow's race." But when you're talking about something that's almost certain not to happen, instead of the indicative you use subjunctive conditional verbs: "She *would go* down in history if she *beat* the world record at tomorrow's race."

See also: conditional, imperative, subjunctive, subjunctive conditional

indirect discourse

Vladimir told me he's allergic to shellfish.

Indirect discourse—also called "indirect quotation"—is language that presents somebody's speech or ideas, but not in his or her own words. When you're writing indirect discourse, you ordinarily don't use quotation marks, so you won't mislead your readers into thinking that you're quoting the other person word for word. Among other changes you might make to the original words, you usually change the pronouns around so that they make grammatical sense in their new context. For instance, suppose Max once told you "I'm allergic to shellfish." In indirect discourse you might say "Max told me he's allergic to shellfish." You can also adjust the tenses—for instance, a present-tense statement that someone made a while ago gets changed to a past-tense statement in indirect discourse, especially if the situation it was describing doesn't apply any more.

- **Other examples:** "The shop owner reminded us that *it was closing time*."

  "The candidate claimed *she would increase public spending without raising taxes*."

  "The Declaration of Independence says that *we all are entitled to the same rights*."

- **Useful tip:** Indirect discourse often begins with the pronoun *that*, but in everyday speech and informal writing it's OK to omit the *that*.

See also: direct discourse, indirect question

indirect object

The waiter brought us the wrong check.

In the sentence above, it's easy to figure out what the grammatical subject is—the waiter is the one who did the bringing, so *waiter* is the subject. And it's not too hard to figure out what the grammatical object of the verb *brought* is—the check is what's being brought, so *check* is the object. But what's the word *us* doing here?

In this sentence, *us* is an indirect object—the person or thing that the action in the sentence is done for or done to. Not every verb has an indirect object—most verbs aren't even *able* to take indirect objects—but when an indirect object is there, you can usually find it immediately following the verb and before the direct object.

- **Other examples:** "He poured *us* some iced tea."

  "Do you always offer *strangers* fashion tips?"

  "I tried to give *my guests* all of my attention."

- **Useful tip:** If you're looking at two nouns or noun phrases that follow a verb and you can't tell whether or not the first is an indirect object, try switching the order and inserting *to* or *for* between them ("He poured some iced tea *for us*" or "I tried to give all of my attention *to my guests*"). If it makes sense rephrased that way, the noun that originally followed the verb was probably an indirect object.

- **Useful tip:** Infinitives and participles, which are made from verbs though they don't count as verbs grammatically, can also have indirect objects, as in the sentence "Why didn't you phone <u>to tell *me*</u> that you were running late?"

See also: complex transitive verb, direct object

indirect question

An indirect question is a question that's phrased as part of a statement (as in the example below) or a demand. Because they aren't phrased as questions, sentences containing indirect questions are punctuated with a period or an exclamation point, not with a question mark.

- If the original question began with a question word like *who, what, where, when, why,* or *how,* that word will also appear in the indirect question.

- If there was no question word in the original question, the indirect question usually begins with *whether* or *if.*

Even an indirect question can get right to the point.

- **Other examples:** "She asked me *what I wanted.*"

  "Sometimes I wonder *whether you're listening to me at all.*"

  "I'm trying to find out *how dolphins use sound to locate fish.*"

- **Useful tip:** When you rephrase a question as an indirect question, you change the sentence structure. Unlike ordinary questions, where the subject comes after *be* or an auxiliary verb ("*Will Jasmine try out* for the play?"), indirect questions put the subject in its usual place before the entire verb phrase ("I haven't heard whether *Jasmine will try out* for the play").

See also: indirect discourse, interrogative

infinitive

Max doesn't realize how much he still has to learn about photography.

The infinitive is a form of the verb that hasn't been changed by any inflections to show tense, number, or person. There are two kinds of infinitives:

1. One is the bare infinitive, the form that verbs appear in when you look them up in dictionaries. Bare infinitives are used in verb phrases together with auxiliary verbs (as in "Max doesn't *realize*").

2. The other kind of infinitive consists of the word *to* followed by a bare infinitive (as in ". . . how much he still has *to learn* about photography").

Since infinitives can't be inflected, they don't count as real verbs when you're trying to figure out whether something is a clause or not. They either form part of a larger verb phrase or act as another part of speech, such as a noun or an adjective.

- **Other examples:** "*To err* is human."

  "This job may *take* all day."

  "We're driving to Florida *to visit* my grandparents."

- **Useful tip:** Though infinitives are usually described as "verbals," not real verbs, they're like verbs in their ability to take direct objects ("to visit *my grandparents*") and even indirect objects ("to write *you* a letter").

See also: bare infinitive, gerund, infinitive phrase, verbal

infinitive phrase

I've never liked to say I'm sorry.

An infinitive phrase is a phrase based on an infinitive that acts as a noun, adjective, or adverb in the grammar of the sentence. For instance, in the sentence above, the object of the verb *liked* is the infinitive phrase "to say I'm sorry," which is based on the infinitive "to say." An infinitive phrase can consist of just the infinitive (usually with *to*), or it can include direct or indirect objects or modifiers.

- When you use an infinitive phrase as an adjective, you don't put it in front of the noun it modifies as if it were an ordinary adjective. That is, you would say "a way *to help*," not "a *to help* way."

- When you use an infinitive phrase as an adverb to modify an adjective, it also usually comes after the adjective it modifies—you'd say "eager *to help*," not "*to help* eager."

- When you use an infinitive phrase as an adverb to modify a verb, it can go after the verb, but it doesn't have to—it can also go at the beginning of the sentence ("*To make an omelet*, you have to break some eggs") or somewhere else in the sentence, usually marked off with commas before and after it ("Vladimir, *to show how agile he is*, performed a double back flip").

- **Other examples:** "*To tease an angry rhinoceros* is not a good idea." (acts as a noun, the grammatical subject of the verb *is*)

  "The night of the party was a night *to remember*." (acts as an adjective modifying the noun *night*)

  "I dance *to express my feelings and personality*." (acts as an adverb modifying the verb *dance*)

See also: participial phrase

inflection

Inflections are changes that you make to words for grammatical reasons. When you change a word according to grammatical rules, you "inflect" it.

- For example, you can make most nouns plural by adding *–s* or *–es* to them (*spoon* becomes *spoons*; *box* becomes *boxes*).

- Likewise, you can inflect verbs to express tense ("The parrots *speak*"; "The parrots *spoke*") or number ("Emma *thinks*"; "Emma and Jasmine *think*") or person ("I *yawn*"; "she *yawns*").

- **Other examples:** *people; people's* (a noun inflected to make it **possessive**)

  hard; harder; hardest (an adjective inflected to show **degree**)

  I; me; mine (a pronoun inflected to show **case**)

- **Useful tip:** Most European languages make use of more inflection than English does. For instance, in French the definite article changes depending on whether the noun it modifies is masculine, feminine, or plural—they say "*le* roi" ("the king"), "*la* reine" ("the queen"), and "*les* rois etreines" ("the kings and queens"). In German, adjectives have endings that show not only whether the noun they modify is masculine, feminine, neuter, or plural, but also whether the noun is a subject, a direct object, an indirect object, or a possessive. But in some other languages, such as Chinese and Vietnamese, inflection plays almost no role—the grammatical relationships are communicated mostly by the order of the words.

See also: finite verb

intensifier

An intensifier, such as *totally* in the cartoon below, is a word (usually an adjective or adverb) that you use to emphasize a point or strengthen the meaning of another word.

Vlad totally needs some new intensifiers.

- **Other examples:** "A modern airplane is a *very* complex piece of technology."

  "Wow! This octopus soup is *really* tasty!"

  "You're *much* too tall to fit into those pants."

- **Caution:** Many of us use intensifiers without thinking about it, as a way of spicing up our speech or writing. But if you use them too much, intensifiers lose their power, so it's a good idea to keep them in reserve for when you need them most. Also, beware of the word *literally*—many people feel that it should never be used as a simple intensifier (as in "My mouth was *literally* burning up after eating those chili peppers"). It's OK to use it when the thing you're describing is an actual fact (as in "A meteorite is a rock that has *literally* fallen out of the sky").

intensive pronoun

I myself occasionally make mistakes.

An intensive pronoun is a pronoun that helps to draw attention to a particular noun or pronoun in a sentence. Intensive pronouns look just like **reflexive pronouns**, but they act differently in the grammar of the sentence. Instead of acting as direct or indirect objects like reflexive pronouns do, intensive pronouns usually appear as an extra pronoun, either at the end of the clause or following the noun or pronoun they refer to. For instance, the pronoun *myself* is a reflexive pronoun in the example above. The grammar of the sentence would be complete without the *myself,* but the extra pronoun helps to draw attention to the fact that the writer or speaker (strange as it may sound) sometimes makes mistakes.

- **Other examples:** "He cooked the meal *himself.*"

  "You *yourself* once told me you were afraid of snakes."

  "The wind whipped the branches, shook the leaves, and even swayed the trunks of the trees *themselves.*"

interjection

Wow! That looks scary!

Interjections are one of the **parts of speech.** An interjection—such as *wow!* in the example above—is a word or set of words that you use just to show how you feel about something. It doesn't have anything to do with the grammar of the sentences around it. It's usually punctuated like a complete sentence, with a period or a question mark or (most often) an exclamation point.

- **Other examples:** "Yikes!"
  "Darn!"
  "Ow!"
  "Eh?"
  "Ah."

- **Exception:** You can use some interjections inside a sentence instead of using them as if they're sentences themselves. When you do this, the interjection will usually be at the beginning of the sentence and will be set off with a comma: "*Oh,* was that your foot I just stepped on?"

interrogative sentence

Have you ever been to Oklahoma City?

An interrogative sentence is a sentence, like the one above, that directly asks a question. There are two kinds of interrogative sentences:

1. The first kind of interrogative asks whether a particular statement is true:

- If the original statement uses a form of the verb *be,* you make it interrogative by putting the verb in front of the subject instead of after it. (For instance, "Philadelphia *was* once the capital of the United States" becomes "*Was* Philadelphia once the capital of the United States?")

- If the original statement uses auxiliary verbs, you make it interrogative by putting its first auxiliary verb in front of the subject instead of after it. ("Pigs *can* fly" becomes "*Can* pigs fly?")

- If the original statement just uses a single verb other than *be,* you make it interrogative by adding *does* or *did* before the subject and replacing the main verb with its infinitive. ("Emma *speaks* Spanish" becomes "*Does* Emma speak Spanish"?)

2. The second kind of interrogative sentence asks for a particular type of information. These interrogatives begin with a question word such as *what* or *when.* For information on how these interrogatives work, see **question word.**

Both kinds of interrogatives are punctuated with a question mark.

See also: declarative sentence, exclamatory interrogation, indirect question, yes-no question

intransitive verb

The shadows lengthen as the afternoon goes on.

An intransitive verb is a verb that doesn't take a direct object. There are few verbs in English that never take a direct object, but it's very common for a verb not to have a direct object in any particular sentence. For instance, the verb *lengthen* is intransitive in the sentence above, but not in a sentence such as "We decided to lengthen our vacation by a few more days," where it takes a direct object (*vacation*).

- **Other examples:** "Wild horses *gallop* over the plains."

  "The vase *shattered* when it hit the floor."

  "I suddenly *sneezed*."

- **Useful tip:** Linking verbs such as *be* or *seem* may seem to take direct objects, but they actually take **subject complements**.

- **Useful tip:** Children's dictionaries often don't tell you whether a verb is intransitive or transitive, but student dictionaries and adult dictionaries usually do, by using abbreviations such as *intr. v.* and *tr. v.* (or *v.i.* and *v.t.*) before the definitions.

See also: complex transitive verb, transitive verb

inversion

Inversion is the act of putting the words of a sentence in a different order than they would usually have. When you do this, you "invert" the usual word order. Inversions are common in old-fashioned writing, especially in poetry. Here are the three most common kinds:

1. reversing the order of a subject and a subject complement ("The night was dark" becomes "Dark was the night")

2. moving a prepositional phrase away from the word it modifies ("We rode out of town" becomes "Out of town we rode")

3. putting an adjective after the noun it modifies ("The city beckoned, with its tall buildings and bright neon" becomes "The city beckoned, with its buildings tall and neon bright").

See also: appositive adjective

irregular plural

Most nouns in English can be made plural by simply adding an *–s* or *–es* to them. But this is not true of every noun. Irregular plurals are plural forms that don't match this pattern. For example, the singular *child* becomes the plural *children*.

The four most common kinds of irregular plurals in English are these:

1. words that take *–es* but also involve changing an *f* to a *v*: *leaf, leaves; shelf, shelves; wolf, wolves*

2. words that become plural by changing their vowel sound: *foot, feet; tooth, teeth; woman, women*

3. words whose plural form is identical to their singular form: *aircraft, moose, species*

4. words that have been adopted, along with special plural forms, from other languages: *cactus, cacti; oasis, oases; phenomenon, phenomena.*

▨ **Useful tip:** Some words can be used with either a regular plural or an irregular plural. For instance, the plural of *hoof* can be either *hoofs* or *hooves.* And the word *medium* takes the plural *mediums* when you use it to mean "people who claim to communicate with the spirits of the dead," but it takes the plural *media* when it means "ways of sending information to large groups of people."

See also: regular plural

irregular verb

Most verbs in English have very predictable forms for their past tense and past participle. For example, you can make *expect* into a past-tense verb or a past participle by adding *–ed* ("I *expected*"; "I have *expected*"). The same is true for verbs such as *cook, touch, walk,* and many others. But for some verbs you don't form the past tense and past participle with *–ed.* These verbs are called irregular verbs. *Break,* for example, is an irregular verb. Its past tense is not "breaked" but *broke,* and its past participle is *broken.*

▨ **Other examples:** *drive; drove; driven*

make; made; made

see; saw; seen

▨ **Useful tip:** The verb *be* is especially irregular—not only does it have unusual past-tense and past-participle forms like *was, were,* and *been,* but even in the present tense it has three completely unrelated forms (*am, are,* and *is*), unlike most other verbs where the present tense is formed from the infinitive, with an added *–s* or *–es* in the third-person singular.

See also: principal parts, regular verb

J

joint possession

How would you make the compound noun phrase "Max and Emma" possessive? Could you just tack on – 's to the end of the phrase ("Max and Emma's")? Or do you need to add – 's to both parts of the phrase ("Max's and Emma's")? The answer depends on whether you're discussing something that belongs to Max and Emma together, or separate things that belong to each of them separately:

● If you're discussing something that belongs to Max and Emma together, it's called joint possession. In cases of joint possession, you only need to add – 's to the second part of the compound noun phrase (*"Max and Emma's* meteorology project won third place at the science fair").

● If you're discussing things that belong separately to Max and Emma, it's not joint possession, and you need to add – 's to both parts of the phrase (*"Max's and Emma's* names are spelled very differently")

■ **Other examples:** "I'm going down to *Paul and Jordana's* house."

"*My aunt and uncle's* children are my cousins."

"It's time to clip *the cat's and the dog's* toenails." (*not* joint possession)

■ **Exception:** If either part of the noun phrase is a pronoun, both should be possessive, whether the situation you're describing is joint possession or not: "Are you coming to *Jasmine's and my* dance recital?"

L

lexical word   See content word

linking verb

Linking verbs are verbs such as *be, become, feel,* or *seem* that you use to describe what the grammatical subject is or how it <u>appears</u> rather than things it actually <u>does</u>. The thing that the subject is described as can be either a noun phrase or an adjective phrase. Either way, it's not considered to be a direct object; instead, it's considered to be a **subject complement**.

Linking verbs don't have superpowers, but they're useful anyway.

- **Other examples:** "That painting *looks* lovely."

  "Russia *is* the largest country on earth."

  "Having lost faith in the revolutionary cause, Benedict Arnold *turned* traitor in 1780."

- **Useful tip:** Since *be* is a linking verb, any pronoun that immediately follows it is a complement of the subject rather than a direct object—which means that it should be a subjective pronoun rather than an objective one. For instance, it's strictly correct to say "it is *I*," not "it is *me*." But very few people follow this rule except in the most formal writing.

See also: action verb, auxiliary verb, complement, subject complement

logical subject   See agent

M

main clause

It shouldn't be very hard if you've been paying attention.

The independent clause in a **complex sentence** is called the main clause of the sentence. For example, the clause "It shouldn't be very hard" is the main clause in the sentence above. You can think

of the main clause as being the base of the sentence, since every complete sentence has to have an independent clause—subordinate clauses can only be part of a sentence if they're attached to a main clause.

■ **Other examples:** "*I ride my bike to school* when the weather is good."

"Because there was no electricity, *we used candles for light.*"

"*Emma likes to cook*, though she isn't very good at it."

■ **Useful tip:** The first independent clause in a compound sentence is also sometimes called the main clause—in fact, some grammar books just define "main clause" as being another term for "independent clause."

main verb

In a verb phrase that includes auxiliary verbs, the main verb is the verb that the auxiliary verbs are attached to. For example, in the verb phrase "will have exploded," the main verb is *exploded*, to which the auxiliaries *will* and *have* are attached. A main verb can be a bare infinitive or a past or present participle, but it isn't a **finite verb**—that is, it doesn't take inflections to show person or number.

● If the main verb is a present participle, you can tell that the verb phrase is in a progressive aspect ("She *was scratching* her head in confusion").

● If the main verb is a past participle following a form of the auxiliary verb *have*, you can tell that the verb phrase is in a perfect aspect ("Apparently the flash flood *had washed* our tent and sleeping bags away").

● If the main verb is a past participle following a form of the auxiliary verb *be,* you can tell that the verb phrase is in the passive voice ("Much to my surprise, he *was offended* by my little joke").

See also: head, passive voice, perfect aspect, progressive aspect, verbal

masculine

The masculine is a grammatical **gender**. Unlike in some languages where every noun has grammatical gender, the masculine in English appears mostly in the use of the subjective personal pronoun *he* , the objective personal pronoun *him*, the reflexive personal pronoun *himself*, and the possessive pronoun and possessive adjective *his*. These words are used mostly to refer to boys and men, though they are also applied to male animals. In addition to these masculine pronouns, there are also a few nouns in English that have both masculine and feminine forms, like *fiancé* and *fiancée* or *god* and *goddess.*

In the past, the various forms of *he* were often used as gender-neutral pronouns—that is, they were used to refer to a person whose gender was unknown, or to refer individually to the members of a group containing both male and female people, as in the sentence "It's important that each student do *his* best." Some writers still feel that using pronouns this way is correct, but many people consider it sexist. It's more acceptable to rephrase the sentence to "It's important that *each* student do *his or her* best" or to "It's important that *all* students do *their* best."

> ■ **Caution:** In everyday speech, almost everyone uses *they* and *them* as a substitute for the gender-neutral *he* and *him*—but in formal writing it is still considered a mistake to use forms of *they* to refer to just one person, as in "The fastest runner will have *their* name inscribed on a plaque." Fortunately, it's usually easy to avoid angering grammar sticklers—all you have to do is rephrase the sentence to something like "The fastest runner will have *his or her* name inscribed on a plaque" or even "The name of the fastest runner will be inscribed on a plaque."

See also: feminine, neuter

mass noun   See noncount noun

modal verb

Those drawings on the cave wall must have been made by prehistoric humans.

Modal verbs are auxiliary verbs, such as *can, may, must, shall,* and *will,* that describe how possible, allowable, or required something is. When you use one of them in a verb phrase along with other auxiliaries such as *be, do,* or *have,* the modal auxiliary comes first and the other auxiliaries come after it, as in the verb phrase "*must* have been made" in the example above.

Modal verbs don't have inflections (that is, they don't take different forms) to express person or number, though most of them do have past-tense forms: *can* becomes *could* in the past tense, *may* becomes *might, shall* becomes *should,* and *will* becomes *would.* These past-tense forms can also be used as subjunctive forms, to express the fact that a particular event isn't the case or isn't likely or possible, as in the sentence "I *would* tell you the answer if I *could.*"

In most cases, modal verbs can be replaced by phrases that have an equivalent meaning. This is especially useful for expressing ideas in the past-perfect and future tenses. For instance, a past-perfect equivalent of "I *can* fly" is "I *had been able to* fly." The future-tense equivalent of "You *must* do the dishes" is "You will *have to* do the dishes" or "You will *be required to* do the dishes."

■ **Useful tip:** The word *ought* behaves much like a modal verb, except that when you use it you usually follow it with *to* and an infinitive, as in "He *ought to know* better than to poke at a hornet's nest."

See also: future tense, subjunctive

modifier

A modifier is a word or a group of words that describes or provides more information about some other word. (In grammar, we say that the modifier "modifies" whatever it's describing or providing information about.) Modifiers come in various forms:

● single words, such as adjectives and adverbs ("the *large* jar"; "slept *soundly*")

● prepositional phrases ("the jar *on the shelf*")

● participial phrases ("the jar *hidden in the back of the refrigerator*")

● whole clauses ("the jar *that is labeled OCTOPUS PUREE*").

Though modifiers often modify nouns, they can also modify verbs, adjectives, adverbs, or even prepositions.

■ **Other examples:** "a *large* snake" (modifies the noun *snake*)

"The rain stopped *suddenly*." (modifies the verb *stopped*)

"an *especially* happy memory" (modifies the adjective *happy*)

"We solved the problem *quite* easily." (modifies the adverb *easily*)

"We're *almost* out of the woods." (modifies the preposition *out of*)

■ **Caution:** When it's not clear what a modifier is meant to be modifying, confusion can result. If you wrote "Flying through the air, I saw a baseball," the reader might wonder what you were doing flying through the air. But a sentence like "I saw a baseball flying through the air" is perfectly clear, because the placement of the phrase *flying through the air* makes it clear just what it modifies (the ball).

See also: adjective, adverb, dangling modifier, prepositional phrase, participial phrase, relative clause

mood

In everyday English, a "mood" is an emotion that you're feeling at some particular time. In grammar, "mood" has a completely different meaning. Grammatical moods are different ways of using verb forms and sentence structures to make it clear whether you're describing events as really happening, speculating about possible events, or making a request or an order.

THIS NEXT TRICK HAS NEVER BEEN DONE BEFORE. IT'S ESSENTIAL THAT YOU BE PERFECTLY STILL. WATCH, AND BE AMAZED!

A good performer sets the right mood—indicative, subjunctive, or imperative.

- **Other examples:** "Jewish religious services *are* conducted at a building called a synagogue." (**indicative** mood—makes a statement)

  "*Had* I learned how to change a tire, we *wouldn't* be stuck by the side of the road now." (**subjunctive** mood—speculates about what would have happened if things were different)

  "*Hand* me that can opener!" (**imperative** mood—makes a request)

- **Useful tip:** Grammatical moods are sometimes called "modes"—a word that is closely related to the adjective *modal*, which you might recognize from the term *modal verb*. In fact, modal verbs often express the same ideas that grammatical moods express—for instance, the idea expressed by using the imperative mood in "*Hand* me that can opener!" can also be expressed by modal verbs in sentences like "*Will* you *hand* me that can opener?" or "You *must hand* me that can opener!"

See also: modal verb

N

negative

Neither flapping your arms nor chirping like a robin will enable you to fly.

A negative is a word or particle that changes the meaning of a sentence (or part of a sentence) by indicating that something is <u>not</u> the case. Negatives can be adverbs ("I *never* eat oysters"), determiners ("Yes, we have *no* bananas"), pronouns ("I opened the beautifully wrapped box, but there was *nothing* inside"), or correlative conjunctions (like *neither* and *nor* in the example sentence above). Or they can be particles that help to form other words, especially contractions ("The lands that Columbus sailed to were*n't* actually part of Asia, but he did*n't* realize that fact.")

■ **Other examples:** "I can*not* tell a lie."

"This wo*n't* hurt a bit."

"*Nobody* has ever made a seventy-yard field goal."

■ **Useful tip:** In everyday life, we use the word "negative" to describe people, attitudes, or statements that are gloomy, unhelpful, or pessimistic. But sentences that use negatives aren't necessarily "negative" in this way. It's easy, in fact, to construct grammatically negative sentences that express cheerful, helpful, or optimistic attitudes: "I've *never* seen such a beautiful sunrise!"

See also: double negative, negative pronoun, negative question

negative pronoun

That flock of crows just seemed to appear out of nowhere.

Negative pronouns are pronouns that include "no" or "not" in their meaning. For instance, in the sentence above, *nowhere* is a negative pronoun that means "*no* place" or "*not* anywhere."

■ **Other examples:** *neither* = "not either"

nobody = "no person" or "not anybody"

none = "not one"

nothing = "no thing" or "not a thing"

- **Useful tip:** Many of the negative pronouns can be used as other parts of speech. For instance, *neither* can be a pronoun ("I tried both keys, but *neither* would unlock the door"), an adjective ("*Neither* gymnast landed the jump perfectly"), or a conjunction ("If Vladimir doesn't go to the party, *neither* will I").

See also: double negative

negative question

Isn't it a nice day?

A negative question is a question that includes a negative word or particle and that expresses an expectation about what the answer will be. For instance, if you ask the negative question "*Isn't* it a nice day?" it usually doesn't mean you're wondering whether it's a nice day or not. Instead, it means you think it's a nice day and you're expecting or hoping that other people agree with you. (If you were really wondering whether it's a nice day or not, you usually wouldn't use a negative question. For instance, if you've just gotten up after sleeping in later than usual, and you haven't looked out the window yet, you might ask someone "Is it a nice day?")

- **Other examples:** "*Isn't* your name Ethelberta?"

  "*Didn't* Galileo discover the moons of Jupiter?"

  "Am I *not* a human being like you?"

- **Useful tip:** You can also use a negative question to make a request. If you ask "Will you invite Jasmine to the party?" it sounds like you're simply asking a question about the future. But if you ask "*Won't* you invite Jasmine to the party?" you express a hope or expectation that the person you're speaking to will invite Jasmine.

See also: rhetorical question

neuter

The neuter is a grammatical **gender.** Unlike in some languages where most nouns—even words for ordinary objects like pencils or books—are categorized as masculine or feminine, in English almost all nouns are grammatically neuter unless they stand for a human being. Neuter nouns can be replaced by the personal pronoun *it* or by the reflexive personal pronoun *itself,* and they can be the antecedents of the possessive adjective *its* (as in "When we approached the *snake, it* coiled *itself* up, hissed, and bared *its* fangs").

Unlike masculine and feminine nouns, which can be antecedents for the possessive pronouns *his* and *hers,* there's no equivalent neuter possessive pronoun—we ordinarily wouldn't say "The maple is my favorite tree, because *its* is the most beautiful foliage in the autumn."

■ **Useful tip:** Most animals are grammatically neuter in English—you might say "The zebra stamped *its* hoofs impatiently" or "I swatted the mosquito before *it* could bite me." But it's very common for people to refer to pets or farm animals by using masculine or feminine pronouns, in sentences such as "Fluffy got too close to the stove and burned *her* whiskers." You can also use masculine or feminine pronouns for wild animals when you're talking specifically about a male or female animal: "The octopus looks for a safe place to lay *her* eggs."

See also: feminine, masculine

nominal

Cats use their tongues to wash themselves.

A nominal is a word, phrase, or clause that acts as a noun in the grammar of the sentence. Nominals can be nouns, pronouns, gerunds, infinitives, noun phrases, or noun clauses, and they can serve any of various purposes in the sentence—they can act as grammatical subjects, as direct or indirect objects of a verb, as complements, or as objects of prepositions or infinitives.

■ **Other examples:** "*Diamonds* are the hardest minerals on earth." (noun, acting as grammatical subject of the verb *are*)

"Cats use their tongues to wash *themselves*." (pronoun, acting as object of the infinitive *wash*)

"A garden is a nice place for quiet *thinking*." (gerund, acting as object of the preposition *for*)

"It's no fun playing against her, because all she wants is to *win*." (infinitive, acting as complement to the phrase "all she wants")

"*An old bicycle with bent spokes, a rusty chain, and defective brakes* might not be the best vehicle for traveling from Maine to Alaska in January." (noun phrase, acting as subject of the verb phrase "might not be")

"I regret *that I spent a month in Venice without learning a word of Italian*." (noun clause, acting as direct object of the verb *regret*)

See also: verbal

nominal clause **See** noun clause

noncount noun

A noun is a noncount noun if it refers to something that can't be counted—not because there are too many of it but because it's

- a substance (like *flour* or *gasoline*)
- a quality (like *creativity* or *honesty*)
- a whole made up of individual things (like *furniture* or *garbage*)
- a field of study or activity (like *biology* or *soccer*)
- a natural phenomenon (like *electricity* or *gravity*)
- an individual name (like *Albert Einstein* or *North Pocatello*).

For instance, you could speak of "an electrician" or "two electric pencil sharpeners" or "47 million electrons," but you couldn't ordinarily speak of "several electricities," so *electricity* is a noncount noun. Noncount nouns (also called "mass nouns") can be used by themselves without definite or indefinite articles, demonstratives, or other **determiners.**

> **Useful tip:** *Much* and *little* are used with noncount nouns, while *many* and *few* are used with count nouns. You would say "How *much* water splashed into the boat?" or "She has very *little* patience" but "How *many* cupcakes did you eat?" or "There are very *few* cupcakes left."

> **Caution:** The comparative *more* and superlative *most* can be used with either count nouns or noncount nouns. But watch out! Many people assume that *less* and *least* work the same way, but the traditional rule is that they can only be used with noncount nouns—for count nouns it's better to use *fewer* and *fewest*. So the sign at the express line at the supermarket should read "10 items or *fewer*," not "10 items or *less*."

See also: count noun

nonrestrictive clause

My ferret, whose name is Nemo, likes to chew on shoelaces.

A nonrestrictive clause is a **subordinate clause** that provides extra information about something or someone you've just mentioned. In the example above, "whose name is Nemo" is a nonrestrictive clause that gives some extra information about the ferret that is the subject of the sentence.

You set off a nonrestrictive clause by putting commas before it and after it. These commas help to tell the reader that the extra information provided isn't absolutely necessary to the meaning of the sentence.

■ **Other examples:** "Golden City, *where I grew up*, gets very little snow."

"Alaska, *which is the largest state*, has a very small population."

"My father, *who was born in China*, is the most patriotic American I know."

■ **Useful tip:** If you can't tell which particular person or thing you're talking about without the information in the added clause—then it's called a **restrictive clause** and you leave out the commas. For instance, if you write, "All students, who are sick, should stay at home," the extra information is essential. After all, you don't want to tell every student to stay home, just the ones who are sick. So you leave out the commas and write "All students who are sick should stay at home."

See also: relative clause, restrictive clause

noun

Nouns, such as *can opener, migration, butterflies, allergy,* and *existence,* are one of the **parts of speech**. They're words that stand for people, places, objects, actions, or ideas. In the grammar of a sentence, a noun can act as the subject of a verb, or it can be an object or a complement.

Learning to recognize nouns is one of the basic skills in understanding grammar. Unfortunately, there's no single trick that will help you recognize nouns wherever you see them, but here are some things you can try:

● If it can be made plural, it could be a noun. You can talk about "one *tree*" or "seven *trees*." But some nouns, such as *togetherness*, can't ordinarily be made plural.

● If you can put *the, a,* or *an* before it, it could be a noun. But some nouns, such as the proper nouns *Shakespeare* and *Chicago*, don't take definite or indefinite articles like these.

● If it can fit into a sentence like "That _____ is nice" or "_____ are confusing," it could be a noun.

■ **Other examples:** "One of the *difficulties* in *training earthworms* to tap-dance is that they have a very poor *sense* of *rhythm*."

"Every ten years the *government* conducts a *census* to find out how many *people* live in the *country*."

"*George III* was the *king of England* at the *time* of the *American Revolution*."

An unknown noun is now a newly known noun!

- **Caution:** Many words can act as different parts of speech depending on the sentence they appear in. For instance, *light* is a noun in "Plants use *light* to create food," but it's an adjective in "Her eyes are *light* blue."

See also: abstract noun, adjectival noun, collective noun, common noun, concrete noun, count noun, gerund, infinitive, nominal, noncount noun, noun clause, noun phrase, proper noun, verbal noun

noun clause

I wonder whose handwriting this is.

A noun clause (also called a "nominal clause") is a kind of **subordinate clause** that acts as a noun in the grammar of the sentence. Like ordinary nouns, noun clauses can play various roles in a sentence:

- They can be grammatical **subjects** ("*What he does in his spare time* is his own business").
- They can be **objects** (like "whose handwriting this is" in the example sentence above).
- They can be **complements** ("The big question is *when we'll stop for lunch*").

- **Other examples:** "She sensed *that the jaguar was ready to pounce*." (direct object of the verb *sensed*)

  "*How you write your name* says a lot about you." (subject of the verb *says*)

  "Vladimir thought with pride about *what he had accomplished*." (object of the preposition *about*)

See also: relative clause

noun phrase

I consider oatmeal the least interesting food in the world.

A noun phrase is a phrase that acts as a noun in the grammar of a sentence. It is made up of an actual noun—or a gerund or an infinitive—along with various modifiers or other parts that are attached to it in some way. Like ordinary nouns, noun phrases can play various roles in a sentence:

- They can be grammatical **subjects** ("*That black dog* looks familiar").

- They can be **objects** ("She handed me *a folded piece of paper*").

- They can be **complements** (like "the least interesting food in the world" in the example sentence above).

- **Other examples:** "a laptop computer with a dead battery" (based around the noun *computer*)

  "a sudden knocking at the door that startled us all" (based around the gerund *knocking*)

  "to give an honest answer to the question" (based around the infinitive *to give*)

See also: nominal

number

In grammar, "number" is what words have when their form makes it clear how many things you are referring to. In some languages, the nouns and verbs have forms that make it clear whether you are referring to one thing, to two things, or to three or more things. In English, we only have different grammatical forms to distinguish between **singular** and **plural** things—if we need to provide more information than that, we do it by putting actual numbers in our noun phrases, as in "*one* cucumber" and "*thirty-two* cucumbers."

Whether something is singular or plural is shown in English grammar in several ways:

- Nouns usually have both singular and plural forms, such as *dictionary* and *dictionaries*.

- Most present-tense verbs have different forms depending on whether their subjects are singular or plural, at least in the third person ("the star *twinkles*"; "the stars *twinkle*"). The verb *be* has different singular and plural forms not only in the third person ("the house *is*"; "the houses *are*") but in the first person as well ("I *am*"; "we *are*") and in the past tense ("I *was*"; "we *were*").

- There are distinct singular and plural pronouns, such as *it* and *they,* which are used depending on whether the antecedent is a singular noun or a plural one.

- Possessive adjectives also have singular and plural forms, both when they're formed from nouns ("the *dog's* owner"; "the *dogs'* owner") and when they're formed from pronouns ("*her* friends"; "*their* friends").

- Demonstratives have singular forms (*this* and *that*) and plural forms (*these* and *those*).

See also: agreement, finite verb, gender, irregular plural, person, plural, regular plural, singular

O

object

Jasmine finally located her lost backpack.

An object is a noun—or a noun phrase or noun clause—that completes a larger part of the sentence. The most common kind of grammatical object is the object of a verb, which usually follows immediately after the verb, helping to complete a **predicate**. For example, in the sentence above, "her lost backpack" is a noun phrase that acts as the object of the verb *located* to complete the predicate "located her lost backpack."

However, an object can also follow an infinitive or a participle, helping to complete a noun phrase or an adjectival or adverbial phrase, as in the sentence "Emma lay awake, enjoying *the sound of the wind in the pines.*" Or it can follow a preposition, helping to complete a prepositional phrase, as in the sentence "We loaded the luggage into *the car.*"

 Useful tip: Not every noun phrase that follows immediately after a verb is an object of that verb. Noun phrases that follow linking verbs such as *be* or *seem* are counted as complements rather than objects.

See also: complement, direct object, indirect object, object of a preposition, subject

object complement

Hot weather makes summer the best season for swimming.

An object complement is a word or phrase that follows a direct object, describing what kind of thing the subject of the verb turns the object into or believes the object to be. For instance, in the sentence "Hot weather makes summer *the best season for swimming,*" the noun phrase "the best season for swimming" is an object complement, because it describes what the direct object (*summer*) is made into by the subject ("warm weather"). An object complement can be a noun, an adjective, or a phrase acting as a noun or adjective.

- **Other examples:** "I consider New Orleans *a lovely city.*" (a noun phrase, acting as a complement to the object New Orleans)

  "We named the new puppy *Max.*" (a proper noun, acting as a complement to the object "the new puppy")

  "The audience found the play *tedious.*" (an adjective, acting as a complement to the object "the play")

- **Useful tip:** It isn't only objects of verbs that can have object complements. Objects of verbals—participles and infinitives—can also have complements, like the phrase "a national monument" in the sentence "Teddy Roosevelt decided <u>to declare</u> the Grand Canyon *<u>a national monument.</u>*"

See also: complex transitive verb, subject complement

objective pronoun

The sudden downpour soaked me from head to toe.

An objective pronoun, like the word *me* in the sentence above, is a pronoun that you use as a grammatical **object**—regardless of whether it's a direct object or an indirect object, and whether it's the object of a verb, of an infinitive, of a participle, or of a preposition. The objective pronouns include the personal pronouns *me, us, you, him, her, it,* and *them,* along with the relative pronouns and question words *whom* and *whomever.*

- **Other examples:** "Slice the onions and separate *them* into rings." (direct object of the verb *separate*)

  "Give *me* the ax." (indirect object of the verb *give*)

  "I'd like to thank my mother and my coach, without *whom* I could never have become the athlete I am today." (object of the preposition *without*)

- **Caution:** Lots of people use *who* and *whoever* as objective pronouns in sentences like *"Who* did you invite to your party?" where according to the traditional rules you should use *whom* instead. For everyday speech and writing, using *who* this way is usually fine. But in formal writing, it's a good idea to use *who* only as a grammatical subject. If you can't tell whether the pronoun is acting as a subject or an object in a particular situation, try this test: Rephrase the sentence, replacing *who* or *whom* with *he* or *him*. If the rephrased sentence works better with *him* ("You invited *him* to your party") than with *he* ("You invited *he* to your party"), it means you need an objective pronoun, so you should use *whom* instead of *who*. If neither sentence sounds right, try the test again, this time using the subjective *they* or the objective *them* in the reworded sentence.

See also: subjective pronoun, reflexive pronoun

object of a preposition

There's some gum on the bottom of your shoe.

An object of a preposition is a noun or noun phrase that combines with a preposition to form a prepositional phrase. For example, in the sentence above, the noun phrase "the bottom of your shoe" is the object of the preposition *on*.

- **Other examples:** "Grunting and scuffling, Vladimir managed to squeeze into *the bears' den*."

  "Don't leave without *saying goodbye*."

  "By *Tuesday*, I have to write a term paper on the behavior of spiders."

- **Useful tip:** The object of a preposition is never the subject or the direct object of a clause, so if you're trying to find the subject or direct object, you can rule out nouns that are obviously part of prepositional phrases. For instance, in "Each *of the fifty states* sends two senators to Congress," you can tell that "the fifty states" can't be the subject, because it's part of the prepositional phrase "of the fifty states." The grammatical subject in this case is the singular pronoun *each*, which is why it takes a singular verb (*sends*) instead of a plural verb (*send*).

▪ **Exception:** For certain informal determiners like *a lot, lots*, and *loads*, the object of the preposition that follows them determines the number of the verb. For example, the sentence "A lot of people watch too much television," the subject is *people* even though it looks like people is the object of a prepositional phrase (*of people*). That's why the verb is plural (*watch*) instead of singular (*watches*).

operator

The first auxiliary verb in a verb phrase is called the operator. For instance, *has* is the operator in "That house <u>*has* been standing</u> for over three hundred years." The operator is important because it's the only **finite verb** in the verb phrase—the only verb that can get changed to show number, person, and tense. The other verbs in the verb phrase—the main verb and any extra auxiliaries such as *have* or *be*—appear either in infinitive form or in participle form to express aspect and voice.

When you make a question out of a declarative clause that contains auxiliary verbs, you move the operator to the beginning of the clause. The rest of the words all stay the same: "<u>*Has*</u> that house <u>been standing</u> for over three hundred years?"

▪ **Other examples:** "The mountain range <u>*was* formed</u> by ancient volcanoes."

"<u>*Must*</u> you <u>be leaving</u> so soon?"

"It looks like I <u>*may* have forgotten</u> my keys again."

▪ **Useful tip:** Though the operator is the only finite verb in the verb phrase, many operators are modal verbs, which don't actually have separate forms for singular and plural or for first, second, and third person. In fact, some modals (*must* and *ought*) don't even have a separate past-tense form.

See also: modal verb

ordinal number

Ordinal numbers are the numbers that you use to describe what order things appear in or happen in—*first, second, third, seventy-fifth*, and so on. Ordinal numbers can act grammatically as adjectives ("July is the *seventh* month of the year"), as adverbs ("August comes *eighth* in the sequence of months"), or as nouns ("September is the *ninth*").

All the ordinal numbers from *third* onward can also express fractional amounts: "Each slice is exactly one *eighth* of the pie." The fraction ½, of course, is not called "one second" but "one half," and the fraction ¼ can be described either as "one fourth" or "one quarter."

> ◼ **Useful tip:** Ordinal numbers can either be spelled out (as in *twelfth*) or written using numerals (as in *12th*). If you're only writing about a few numbers, and if those numbers are fairly small, it's traditional to spell them out: "Our eggplant took *third* prize at the county fair." But if some of the numbers you're writing about are larger numbers, it's a good idea to use numerals: "Unfortunately, you are only the *999th* person to visit our store today, so you don't win the grand prize."

See also: cardinal number

P

parallel construction

Parallel construction is a way of setting up your sentences so that several different parts have a similar grammatical structure. For instance, Julius Caesar's famous boast "I *came*, I *saw*, I *conquered*" uses parallel construction to create a dramatic effect; it wouldn't have been so memorable if he had said "After I got there I looked around, and then we fought the enemy and beat them." (Actually, being Roman, Caesar spoke Latin, so what he actually said was "Veni, vidi, vici." But that uses parallel construction too.)

> ◼ **Other examples:** "The further Emma climbed, the narrower the tree's branches became."
>
> "It was a pleasant landscape of light-green fields and dark-green woods."
>
> "Annalena, who had never acted before, who disliked public speaking, and who was shy around strangers, performed her role so well that she got a standing ovation."

> ◼ **Useful tip:** When you list two or more things, actions, or qualities, it often sounds better if you list them using similar grammatical structures. Rather than saying "Three things I like about summer vacations are

beaches, <u>camping with my family</u>, and <u>that I can sleep late on Mondays</u>," you might want to use a parallel construction: "Three things I like about summer vacations are <u>relaxing at the beach</u>, <u>camping with my family</u>, and <u>sleeping late on Mondays</u>."

Vlad's parallel construction is a little off.

parenthetical expression

Maria Skłodowska, the Polish scientist also known by the name Marie Curie, pioneered the study of radioactivity.

A parenthetical expression is a construction that adds extra information to a sentence—information that isn't a necessary part of the sentence's meaning, in a construction that isn't a necessary part of the sentence's grammar. For instance, in the sentence above, the noun phrase "the Polish scientist also known by the name Marie Curie" is a parenthetical expression. The sentence would still make perfect sense and would still be perfectly grammatical without it, though it would provide less information: "Maria Skłodowska pioneered the study of radioactivity." Despite its name, a parenthetical expression doesn't necessarily involve parentheses. Most often, as in the example above, a parenthetical expression is marked off with commas before and after it. But you can also use dashes or, yes, even parentheses to mark it off.

▪ **Other examples:** "Apples—*my favorite fruit, by the way*—don't ripen until the end of the summer."

"Vladimir, *of course*, knows how to tie his shoes."

"My friend (*you remember her, I'm sure—the one who tap-danced in a sequined suit at the talent show*) says that she's thinking of studying karate."

Useful tip: If a parenthetical expression is a word, phrase, or clause that modifies something else in the sentence, you can use any of the three kinds of punctuation marks described above to set it off from the rest of the sentence. If the parenthetical expression is a whole sentence, you should use dashes or parentheses, not commas, before it and after it.

See also: appositive, nonrestrictive clause

parse

To "parse" a sentence is to look at it and figure out how its grammar works—which words are acting as which parts of speech, which nouns are subjects and which are objects, what's being modified by what, what nouns the pronouns are standing for, and so on. If you can read and speak English, you already know how to do this, even if you don't know you know it—every time you read or hear a sentence, you parse it without thinking about it, in order to understand what it's saying. But even native speakers can make mistakes in their English. The point of studying grammar is to learn the names for different grammatical ideas so that you can learn to recognize and fix grammatical mistakes.

participial noun   See gerund

participial phrase

*The car's engine suddenly died,
giving off a cloud of black smoke.*

A participial phrase is a phrase that's based on a past or present participle and that acts as an adjective or adverb in the grammar of the sentence, modifying some other part of the sentence. For instance, in the sentence above, the phrase "giving off a cloud of black smoke" is a participial phrase—based on the present participle *giving*—that acts as an adverb to modify the verb *died*, telling more about the dying of the engine.

Other examples: "The cookies, *burnt black around the edges*, didn't look very appealing."

"*Swatting furiously* and *using rather bad language*, we desperately tried to outrun the mosquitoes."

"Every night I sing lullabies to my baby brother, *that being the only way to get him to fall asleep.*"

■ **Useful tip:** Since participles are made from verbs, they can take direct or indirect objects, complements, or even subjects, just as if they were actual verbs. But the participle in a participial phrase isn't a **finite verb**, so it doesn't count toward making a complete clause or a complete sentence.

See also: infinitive phrase

participle

If you had to sit through such a boring movie, you'd be as bored as I am!

A participle, such as *boring* or *bored*, is a word that is made from a verb but can act as any of various parts of speech:

● It can act as an adjective, as *boring* and *bored* do in the example above.

● It can act as a noun ("Emma's *singing* always puts her baby brother to sleep"). In this case it is called a **gerund**.

● It can act as part of a verb phrase after one or more auxiliary verbs ("I <u>should have *brought*</u> you flowers when you were in the hospital"). When a participle is used in a verb phrase like this, it helps to show grammatical **aspect** or **voice**.

■ **Other examples:** "Let *sleeping* dogs lie."

"The *unexamined* life is not worth living."

"We hold these truths to be self-evident: that all men are *created* equal; that they are *endowed* by their creator with certain unalienable rights; that among these are life, liberty, and the pursuit of happiness."

See also: infinitive, participial phrase, passive voice, past participle, perfect aspect, present participle, progressive aspect, verbal

particle

I'm afraid of cats.

A particle is a word—usually a short word like *of* in the example above—that never changes form, regardless of how it fits in the grammar of a sentence. It has no singular or plural number; no past, present, or future tense; no case, mood, aspect, or voice; no first-person, second-person, or third-person form; and no comparative or superlative. Many particles function as adverbs or prepositions, but (like *up* in "Irregular verbs have always tripped me up") they don't have the normal meaning that we associate with these words. In fact it's often hard to say exactly what a particular particle means.

■ **Other examples:** "That's *not* fair!"
"Relax, *and* have some iced tea."
"*The* sun is setting."
"I *too* am left-handed."

See also: function word

part of speech

The parts of speech are different kinds of words, divided into categories based on what they're doing in the grammar of a sentence. Every word in a sentence belongs to one of these nine parts of speech: *noun, verb, adjective, adverb, preposition, pronoun, conjunction, article,* or *interjection.* It's important to understand that the same word might act as different parts of speech in different sentences—or even at different places in the same sentence. And it's also possible for a group of words (a phrase or a clause) to work together as if they were a single part of speech.

■ **Useful tip:** In a dictionary entry, a word's part of speech is usually written as an abbreviation like "*n.*" or "*adj.*" just before the definition. If the word has more than one meaning, the different definitions will usually be organized according to what part of speech they correspond to.

See also: adjective, adverb, article, conjunction, interjection, noun, preposition, pronoun, verb

passive voice

The code was broken by a team of mathematicians.

The passive is one of the two grammatical voices in English. It's the voice that you use in constructing sentences like "I've been robbed!" or "These posters were created by Jordana." Ordinarily, when you're describing people's actions or everyday events, you use a sentence structure where the person (or thing) that is responsible for the action is also the grammatical subject, and where the person (or thing) that something happens to is the grammatical object: "A team of mathematicians broke the code." In the passive voice, the one that something happens to is the grammatical subject, and the one that is responsible for the action often appears in a prepositional phrase starting with *by*: "The code was broken by a team of mathematicians." Notice that there's also a change in the form of the verb—the original verb (*broke*) changes to its past-participle form (*broken*) and also pairs up with a form of *be* (*was*).

- **Other examples:** "The child in the story *was raised* by wolves."

  "These pencils *have been chewed on* by somebody."

  "I hope to *be elected* class president."

- **Useful tip:** When it doesn't really matter who is doing the action in the sentence—or when you don't know who's doing the action—you can use the passive voice without the *by* phrase: "The wheel was invented many thousands of years ago."

- **Caution:** The passive voice is perfectly grammatical, but it's a bad idea to use it too much. For one thing, putting things in the passive can make the grammar more complex and harder to read. For another, people sometimes use the passive without the *by* phrase to try to avoid the blame for something, so the passive can seem sneaky and defensive. (Think of the difference in tone between "Your notebook *was taken* from your locker" and "*I took* your notebook from your locker.") Many word-processing programs have grammar-checkers that identify and point out passive-voice constructions so that you can decide whether you really need them.

See also: active voice

past participle

The past participle is one of the **principal parts** of a verb. You usually produce past participles by adding a suffix to the original verb. For all regular verbs, you make the past participle by adding *–ed*, just like you do when you're making the ordinary past tense form of the verb (*look* becomes *looked*). But for many irregular verbs, you add the suffix *–en* instead (*fall* becomes *fallen*). For other irregular verbs, you make the past participle by just changing the vowel sound of the original verb (*sing* becomes *sung*), by changing the vowel and adding a suffix (*break* becomes *broken*), or by changing the vowel and the consonants at the end of the word (*think* becomes *thought*). There are even a few verbs (such as *cut, cast,* and *split*) whose past participle forms are identical to both the present tense and past tense forms.

Past participles have three main uses:

1. After a form of *be* in a verb phrase, the participle shows that the verb is in the passive voice: "I <u>was *chosen*</u> to represent our school in the spelling bee."

2. After a form of *have* in a verb phrase, the participle shows that the verb is in the perfect aspect: "Emma <u>has *waited*</u> her whole life to see a solar eclipse."

3. In other constructions, the participle acts as an adjective, showing that the thing it modifies was the direct or indirect object of a particular action. For instance, the past participle *broken* in "a *broken* window" makes it clear that something or someone broke the window.

See also: irregular verb, participial phrase, passive voice, perfect aspect, present participle, regular verb

past perfect

The tracks showed that some animal had walked down the path before us.

The past perfect is a form of the verb that combines the past **tense** and perfect **aspect**. You use it when you're discussing some point of time in the past when something had already happened. For instance, in the sentence above, the verb phrase "had walked" is in the past perfect, because it's describing a time in the past (the moment the tracks were discovered) when some other event (the animal's walking down the path) had already happened.

The past perfect is always formed by the past-tense auxiliary verb *had*, followed by the past participle of another verb. That other verb can be the main verb of the verb phrase, as in the example above, or it can be the auxiliary verb *been* if the verb phrase is in the passive **voice** ("My luggage *had been forgotten*") or if it involves the progressive aspect in addition to the perfect aspect ("I *had been thinking* of something else").

■ **Other examples:** "By the age of ten Vladimir *had* already *gone* to seventeen skateboard competitions." (past perfect)

"After searching the entire house for my glasses, I realized I *had been wearing* them the whole time." (past perfect with progressive aspect)

"A row of cornstalks now stood where the seeds *had been planted* in the spring." (past perfect in passive voice)

■ **Useful tip:** The past perfect is sometimes called the "pluperfect," especially in older grammar books.

See also: compound tense

past progressive

Emma was sniffling when the movie ended.

The past progressive is a form of the verb that combines the past **tense** and progressive **aspect.** You use it when you're discussing some point of time in the past when something was currently going on. For instance, in the sentence above, the verb phrase "was sniffling" is in the past progressive, because it's describing a time in the past (when the movie ended) when some other event (Emma's sniffling) was happening.

The past progressive is always formed by the past-tense auxiliary verb *was* or *were*, followed by the present participle of another verb. That other verb can be the main verb of the verb phrase, as in the example above, or it can be the auxiliary verb *being* if the verb phrase is in the passive voice ("We walked into a clearing where a pile of leaves and brush *was being burnt*").

■ **Other examples:** "I couldn't sleep because the moonlight *was shining* so brightly through the window."

"I *was* just *looking* for you."

"While the prescription *was being filled*, we wandered in the aisles of the pharmacy." (past progressive in passive voice)

See also: compound tense

past tense

The stock market crash in 1929 triggered the Great Depression.

The past tense is a form of the verb that you use to discuss events that have already happened. For instance, in the sentence above, the verb *triggered* is in the past tense, because it describes an event (the start of the Great Depression) as something that happened in the past (1929).

When you make a past-tense sentence using a verb phrase with auxiliary verbs, only the first auxiliary verb changes its form—you'd change "I do remember" to "I did remember," not "I did remembered."

- **Other examples:** "We *returned* from our vacation late last night."

  "*Did* you *turn* off the oven?" (verb phrase combining the past-tense *did* with the infinitive *turn*)

  "I *was born* in Milwaukee" (passive verb phrase combining the past-tense was with the past participle *born*)

- **Caution:** You probably already know that most verbs get an *–ed* suffix in their past-tense forms. But many of the *–ed* words that look like past-tense verbs are actually past participles—they can be part of a larger verb phrase with auxiliaries, or they can act as adjectives, but they don't count as **finite verbs**—they don't make a clause a clause.

See also: future tense, irregular verb, past perfect, past progressive, present tense, regular verb

perfect aspect

The perfect is one of the possible **aspects** of a verb—that is, it's a way of describing the relation between a particular action and a particular point in time. You use the perfect aspect when you want to describe an event as being already completed by a particular point or as continuing up until a particular point. For instance, the verb phrase "has been" is in the perfect aspect in the dialogue below, because it expresses the idea that the brokenness of the computer has continued up to the present moment. You form the perfect aspect of a verb by combining a form of *have* with a past participle of the verb.

Emma thinks of a (grammatically) perfect excuse.

- **Other examples:** "It *has snowed* for two days now."

  "The site where the Pilgrims built the colony of Plymouth *had* once *been* a Native American village."

  "By sunset the rising tide *will have erased* most of the footprints on the beach."

See also: future perfect, past perfect, present perfect, progressive aspect

periodic sentence

If you ask me nicely enough, and if you promise not to pester me ever again, and if you give me half of your sandwich first . . . I might give you half my cookie.

A periodic sentence is a long sentence whose grammatical structure isn't complete until the very end. Periodic sentences use the power of grammar to hold the listener's attention. For example, the sentence above begins with a subordinate clause starting with *if.* A subordinate clause can't stand by itself without an independent clause, so you're left waiting for the independent clause that will complete the grammar of the sentence. Because the speaker adds several more subordinate clauses before getting to the independent clause, you're left in suspense until the very end.

You can also create periodic sentences by using repeating phrases: "Out in the great north woods, up in the land of the pine and the spruce, in the land of starry nights and northern lights, in the land of the moose and the loon, beside the wave-lapped shore of a lake, stood a small log cabin."

- **Useful tip:** Periodic sentences can be a useful way to add flavor to your writing, but with periodic sentences—just like with spices—a little bit can go a long way. If every sentence you write is a periodic sentence, your readers will soon get tired and frustrated. Use them, but use them sparingly!

periphrastic

A construction is called periphrastic if it uses extra words to say what could ordinarily be said more simply. There are two types of periphrastic constructions in grammar that are worth knowing about:

1. A periphrastic **genitive** construction uses the extra word *of* instead of using a possessive ending like – *'s*. For example, "the house of my friend" is a periphrastic way of saying "my friend's house." Most of the time these two kinds of constructions are equally acceptable, but in some contexts it makes a difference which you use. "A picture of my friend" means that the friend is depicted in the picture, not that the friend owns the picture.

2. A periphrastic **comparative** or **superlative** construction uses the extra word *more* or *most* instead of using the suffix *–er* or *–est*. For instance, you might say "more shallow" or "most shallow" instead of *shallower* or *shallowest*. Though there are many words which can be made comparative or superlative using either of these constructions, longer adjectives usually take a periphrastic construction (you'd say "more reasonable," not "reasonabler"), while adverbs and very short adjectives usually sound awkward in periphrastic constructions (you'd say "darker," not "more dark").

person

In everyday life, *person* refers to a human being. It has a similar meaning in grammar, too, except that in grammar it refers not to the people themselves but rather the category that they belong to in terms of the sentence. In English the only words that have grammatical person are pronouns, verbs, and possessive adjectives, and they fall into three separate categories:

1. the speaker of the sentence (**first person**)

2. the person or people being spoken to (**second person**)

3. the person, people, or thing being spoken about (**third person**).

English pronouns change their form for each of these three categories. For example, the subjective pronoun is *I* (singular) or *we* (plural) in the first person, *you* (both singular and plural) in the second person, and *he, she,* or *it* (singular) or *they* (plural) in the third person. Objective pronouns have similar changes (*me, us,* etc.), as do the possessive adjectives (*my, our,* etc.). Most English verbs change their form only in the third-person singular in the present tense, though the verb *be* has separate forms for first-person singular (*am*) and third-person singular (*is*), with the remaining singular and plural forms all being the same (*are*).

See also: agreement, gender, number

personal pronoun

She may not look it, but she's the state Ping-Pong champion.

The personal pronouns, such as *we, him, theirs,* and *ourselves,* are pronouns that have grammatical **person**—that is, they're pronouns that you use to make it clear whether you're referring to yourself, to someone else, or to your listener or reader. In addition to showing what person you're referring to, personal pronouns can be inflected to show **number** and **gender**, and they fall into four basic categories depending on the grammatical role they're playing in the sentence (that is, their **case**):

1. They can act as subjects, like the word *she* in the example sentence above.

2. They can act as objects ("A hornet stung *her* on the nose").

3. They can act as objects but also show that the object is the same as the subject of the sentence ("She told *herself* there was no need to be nervous").

4. They can show that something belongs to something or someone ("*Hers* is the messiest locker in the school").

■ **Caution:** Just because personal pronouns have "personal" in their names and they have grammatical "person," don't assume that pronouns only count as personal pronouns if they actually refer to people. The pronouns *it* and *itself*, for instance, are used to refer to objects, animals, and ideas, and the pronouns *they, them, theirs,* and *themselves* can refer either to people ("The guests put on their coats as *they* left the house") or to other things ("These pens may look cool, but *they* don't write clearly"). All of these pronouns are personal pronouns.

See also: objective pronoun, possessive pronoun, reflexive pronoun, subjective pronoun

phrasal verb

On a whim, Jasmine decided to take up kickboxing.

A phrasal verb is a phrase that consists of a verb combined with an adverb, such as "take up" in the sentence above. The adverb in a phrasal verb is always a word—such as *up, out, in,* or *through*—that could be a preposition in another sentence. Like **idioms**, phrasal verbs have special meanings that aren't necessarily clear based on the words themselves.

(What does "taking up" have to do with *taking*? What does it have to do with the direction *up*?) The verb and adverb are ordinarily placed together, but when the phrasal verb has a very short object—and especially when the object is a pronoun—the adverb typically comes after the object, as in the sentence "Those shoes won't fit well until you *break* them *in*."

▪ **Other examples:** "The umpire *called* the game *off* when it began to rain."

"I don't want to *wear out* my welcome."

"My request for a second piece of pie was *turned down*."

▪ **Caution:** Sometimes it's hard to tell whether a word is part of a phrasal verb or not. In the sentence "We *ran up* a huge cell phone bill in April," *up* is an adverb in the phrasal verb "ran up," but in the sentence "We ran *up the road* to Max's house," *up* is a preposition in the prepositional phrase "up the road."

▪ **Useful tip:** Most good dictionaries include phrasal verbs, often listing them at the end of the entry that defines the verb itself. For instance, you might look for the meaning of "sit out" near the end of the entry for *sit*, and you might find an explanation of "stand for" near the end of the entry for *stand*.

phrase

Giraffes with short necks don't like tall trees.

A phrase is a set of words working together as a unit. It isn't a whole sentence. Some phrases act as nouns. Some phrases act as verbs, adjectives, adverbs, prepositions, or conjunctions. For instance, in the sentence above, we can call "giraffes with short necks" a phrase, because in this sentence it works just like a single noun. We could replace it with the single word "giraffes," and we'd wind up with a sentence that would still be a sentence, though it might not make perfect sense: "*Giraffes* don't like tall trees."

▪ **Other examples:** "In the Middle Ages, the sun *was thought to revolve* around the earth." (acts as a verb)

"*Whistling her favorite song*, Emma strolled downtown." (acts as an adjective)

"She had barely gotten *as far as* Third Avenue when her shoelace broke." (acts as a preposition)

Useful tip: Phrases can be very short, like the verb phrase "can be." Or they can be very long, like the noun phrase "the chalk in the fingers of the teacher who is writing a very difficult math problem on the blackboard." Long phrases are often made up of lots of smaller phrases. They may even have whole clauses inside them. But they're not whole sentences—a long phrase is not a sentence any more than a noun or an adjective by itself is a sentence.

See also: adverbial phrase, noun phrase, verb phrase, participial phrase, prepositional phrase

pluperfect   See past perfect

plural

Words that refer to a group of more than one person, thing, or idea are said to be plural in **number.** Several different parts of speech can be plural:

- Nouns are the most obvious example. The noun *bears*, for instance, is the plural form of *bear*.

- Verbs take a plural form whenever their grammatical subject is plural. Much of the time, the plural form is identical to the singular form ("First one grizzly bear *awoke*. Then two more grizzly bears *awoke*"). But third-person verbs in the present tense have different singular and plural forms ("First one grizzly bear *growls* angrily. Then two more grizzly bears *growl* angrily").

- Pronouns take a plural form whenever they stand for a plural antecedent ("The angry *grizzly bears* growled when *they* sensed an intruder in their den").

- Possessives take a plural form whenever the noun or pronoun they're formed from (<u>not</u> the noun they modify!) is plural: "Hearing growling all around him, Vladimir backed quickly out of the *grizzly bears'* den."

- Demonstratives take a plural form whenever they refer to a plural noun ("He felt lucky to be far away from *those* angry *bears*").

See also: agreement, irregular plural, regular plural, singular

positive degree

The positive degree is a way of using an adjective or adverb when you just want to describe something as having a quality, without comparing it to other things that have more or less of that quality. The positive degree is the ordinary form of an adjective or adverb, such as *weird*, *inflatable*, *purple*, or *fortunately*.

> ■ **Useful tip:** Dictionaries usually define adjectives and adverbs at the entry for the positive degree form. If a word also has comparative and superlative forms, they're usually listed in that same entry, not in their own entry. In a few cases, when the different forms are spelled very differently (*much*, *more*, and *most*, for instance), each gets its own entry.

See also: comparative degree, periphrastic, superlative degree

possessive

The possessive is the grammatical form that shows that something is in the **genitive** case. Most of the time, you use possessive forms when you're describing somebody as owning (or "possessing") something, as in the sentence "That quartz crystal is the centerpiece of *Emma's* rock collection."

- You form the grammatical possessive of most singular nouns by adding the suffix –*'s* ("*my English class's* group project").

- Plural nouns that already end in –*s* become possessive by just adding an apostrophe at the end ("the two *teams'* goalies").

- Plural nouns that don't end in –*s* are made possessive by the same rule as for singular nouns ("the *fungi's* spores").

Once a noun has been made possessive, it and any modifiers in front of it act together as an adjective in the grammar of the sentence, modifying the thing that's being "possessed."

Pronouns can be made into possessive adjectives as well. Personal pronouns and the pronoun *who* have special possessive adjective forms that don't use apostrophes (*my, our, your, his, her, its, their, whose*), but other kinds of pronouns can be made possessive by following the usual rule for nouns ("*somebody's* lunch"; "*others'* opinions of him").

> ■ **Caution:** Though in everyday life the verb *possess* usually means "to own," the possessive form in grammar often describes relationships other than ownership: "*the test's* difficulty," "*Vladimir's* happiest experience," "*the emperor's* lifelong enemy."

Jasmine is very possessive, even about her mistakes.

See also: joint possession, possessive pronoun

possessive pronoun

He accidentally walked away with my phone, and I walked away with his.

A possessive pronoun, such as *his* in the example above, is a pronoun in the **genitive** case. You use possessive pronouns as a replacement for noun phrases that involve possessive adjectives. In this case, *his* is a replacement for the noun phrase "his phone." The possessive pronouns look very much like possessive adjectives, but with a few differences:

possessive pronoun	possessive adjective
mine	*my*
ours	*our*
yours	*your*
his	*his*
hers	*her*
its [very rarely used]	*its*
theirs	*their*
whose	*whose*

- **Other examples:** "Your house may be air-conditioned, but *ours* is closer to the town swimming pool."

"*Whose* do you like best of all the proposals?"

"Can I borrow your pencil? I've lost *mine*."

See also: possessive

predicate

Max has been trying to open that bag of chips for at least five minutes.

A predicate is a part of a sentence that consists of a verb and all of the objects, complements, and adverbs that go along with that verb. You can think of a predicate as being a description of what the subject of the sentence does or is.

Every sentence contains at least one predicate, because every clause contains at least one verb and every sentence contains at least one clause. Traditionally, every word in a one-clause sentence is considered to be either part of the subject or part of the predicate. In the example above, *Max* is the subject and the rest of the sentence is the predicate.

■ **Other examples:** "This cheese *smells like old socks*."

   "*Are* penguins *found at the North Pole?*"

   "Not one of the students in the entire class *was able to diagram that fiendishly complex sentence without making a mistake or at least bursting into tears in the process.*"

■ **Exception:** Imperative sentences often don't mention the subject at all, since imperatives are always asking or ordering the reader or listener to do something and since most of the time people know when they're being talked to. So lots of imperative sentences consist of nothing but a predicate: "Beware of the dog!"

See also: compound predicate, predicate adjective, predicate nominative, subject

predicate adjective

The wall sounded hollow when we knocked on it.

A predicate adjective, like the word *hollow* in the sentence above, is an adjective that acts as a **complement** to a subject or object in a sentence. The predicate adjective describes a quality of the subject or object it's acting as a complement to—in this case, it describes how the subject ("the wall") sounds.

■ **Other examples:** "Typically, nighttime is *dark*." (describing the subject *nighttime*)

"You seem a little *worried*." (describing the subject *you*)

"The Supreme Court declared the new law *unconstitutional*." (describing the object "the new law")

- **Useful tip:** A predicate adjective doesn't have to be a single word. It can also be a phrase (as in "The jury found me *not guilty by reason of insanity*") or a clause (as in "She looked *as if she'd seen a ghost*") acting as an adjective.

See also: object complement, predicate nominative, subject complement

predicate nominative

A predicate nominative, like the phrases "a good student," "a down-to-earth-person," "a loyal friend," and "our next class president" in the cartoon below, is a noun or noun phrase that acts as a **complement** to a subject in a sentence. The predicate nominative tells what kind of thing the subject is, or what it becomes, or what it seems to be. In this case, all of the phrases describe what the subject (Emma or "she") is or should be.

A predicate nominative nomination.

- **Other examples:** "Earth is *the third planet from the sun*." (tells what the subject, *earth*, is)

  "That rock resembles *a sheep*." (tells what the subject, *that rock*, seems to be)

  "Snowball won't remain *a kitten* forever." (tells what the subject, *Snowball*, is—at least for now)

See also: object complement, predicate adjective, predicate objective, subject complement

predicate objective

I often find your behavior a bit of a mystery.

A predicate objective, like the phrase "a bit of a mystery" in the sentence above, is a noun or noun phrase that acts as a **complement** to an object in a sentence. The predicate objective tells what kind of thing the object is, what it becomes, what it seems to be, or what someone declares it to be. In this case, "a bit of a mystery" is what the object (your behavior) seems to be.

- **Other examples:** "I've always considered Vladimir *my friend.*" (tells what the object *Vladimir* is, in the speaker's opinion)

  "Surprisingly, the electric paper clip has not made its inventor *a millionaire.*" (tells what the object *its inventor* could be, but isn't)

  "Despite the kitten's black fur, we named her *Snowball.*" (tells what the object *her* has been declared to be)

See also: object complement, predicate adjective, predicate nominative, subject complement

prefix

The arid climate of the Sahara becomes semiarid as you go south into the Sahel region.

A prefix consists of one or more syllables that you attach to the beginning of a word (or to a **root** or **stem**) to produce a new word with a different meaning. For instance, in the sentence above, the adjective *semiarid* is formed by adding the prefix *semi–* to the adjective *arid*. As in this example, adding a prefix to a word usually doesn't change the part of speech the word belongs to.

- **Other examples:** *anti–* as in *antimatter* or *antisocial*
  pre– as in *preheat* or *preview*
  super– as in *superhero* or *supermarket*

- **Useful tip:** Nearly all of the most common prefixes in English are borrowed from Latin or Greek. Exceptions to this rule include *un-* and several prefixes that are derived from English prepositions: *down– out–, over–, up–,* and so on.

See also: affix, suffix

preposition

There's a spider crawling up your leg.

Prepositions, such as *after, between, for, of, until,* and *up,* are one of the **parts of speech.** You use them to describe the relationship between one noun phrase and another, or the relationship between a verb and a noun phrase—often relationships having to do with space and time, but not always.

- **Other examples:** "The candles *on* the table flickered gently." (describes the relationship in space between the *candles* and the *table*)

  "I'd like to be a dairy farmer, but I'd hate waking *before* dawn to milk the cows." (describes the relationship in time between the *waking* and *dawn.*)

  "The novel is *about* a computer that takes over the world." (describes what the *novel* has to do with the *computer*)

- **Useful tip:** There are only a few dozen prepositions in English. In fact, you probably already know almost all of them. But not everything that looks like a preposition actually is one. Many words that can be prepositions can also be adverbs. For instance, *up* is a preposition in a sentence like "There's a spider crawling *up* your leg," because it explains the relationship between the *crawling* and the *leg.* But *up* is an adverb in a sentence like "A strange noise caused me to look *up,*" because it just modifies the verb *look.*

See also: complex preposition, object of a preposition, phrasal verb, prepositional phrase

prepositional phrase

Vladimir's sunglasses sank into the deep end of the pool.

A prepositional phrase is a phrase (such as "into the deep end of the pool" in the sentence above) that contains one or more prepositions (like *into*) followed by a noun or noun phrase (like "the deep end of the pool"). Prepositional phrases serve two main purposes:

1. They can act as adverbs, usually to modify a verb ("A jaguar <u>lurked *on the branch overhead*</u>").

2. They can act as adjectives, either directly modifying a noun ("Fortunately, the <u>jaguar *on the branch overhead*</u> was asleep") or acting as a subject or object **complement** ("We were safe as long as the jaguar

was _on the branch overhead_ and not _on top of us_").

- **Other examples:** "When I am _in Paris_ I will visit the Eiffel Tower." (acts as an adjective complement to the subject _I_)

  "Emma talks _in her sleep._" (acts as an adverb modifying _talks_)

  "Cuba is an island _south of Florida._" (acts as an adjective modifying _island_)

- **Useful tip:** There are two ways to take a prepositional phrase from one sentence (like "We stood _on the sidewalk_") and rephrase it so that the noun in the prepositional phrase becomes the subject or direct object of its own sentence. You can just switch it around so that the noun from the prepositional phrase comes before the subject and verb of the old sentence, with or without the pronoun _that_ or _whom_ ("The sidewalk [that] _we stood on_"). Or you can put the noun from the prepositional phrase first, followed by the preposition, then by the pronoun _which_ or _whom_, and then by the old subject and verb ("The sidewalk _on which we stood_"). In both of these sentence structures the old subject and verb are now part of a subordinate clause.

See also: object of a preposition, relative clause

present participle

Lots of people carry a book to the beach; Emma walked onto the sand carrying twelve.

The present participle is one of the **principal parts** of a verb. You usually make present participles by adding the suffix _–ing_ to the original verb—as with the example above, in which the infinitive verb _carry_ becomes the participle _carrying_. Present participles have three main uses:

1. After a form of _be_ in a verb phrase, the participle shows that the verb is in the progressive aspect ("I _am hoping_ to climb Mt. Everest before I turn eighty").

2. A present participle can act as a noun: ("The _chirping_ of the tree frogs kept me awake all night").

3. In other constructions, the participle acts as an adjective. Most often the participle shows that the thing it modifies is doing something. For instance, the present participle _dripping_ in "a dripping faucet" expresses the idea that the faucet itself drips. But other times the participle shows what something is for ("_dining_ room"; "_bathing_ suit").

- **Exception:** In a few everyday phrases, such as "*hopping* mad" or "filthy *stinking* rich," the present participle acts as an adverb to modify an adjective.

- **Useful tip:** If the verb ends in a silent *e,* you drop the *e* when you add –*ing* (*chase* becomes *chasing*). If the verb ends in a single consonant other than *x* and the consonant has a single short vowel before it, the consonant gets doubled (*set* becomes *setting*).

See also: gerund, participial phrase, past participle, progressive aspect

present perfect

Max has waited all summer for the opening of the new water park.

The present perfect is a form of the verb that combines the present **tense** and perfect **aspect**. It serves two main purposes:

1. You use it to describe something that happened or began sometime in the past and is still the case now. For instance, in the sentence above, the present perfect verb phrase "has waited" shows that the waiting began in the past and is still going on.

2. You use it to describe something that happened in the past and isn't happening now but could possibly happen again in the future ("I *have been* to Whitneyville a few times").

You form the present perfect by combining the past-tense auxiliary verb *have* or *has* with the past participle of another verb. That other verb can be the main verb of the verb phrase, as in the examples above, or it can be the auxiliary verb *been* if the verb phrase is in the passive **voice** ("My lunch *has been stolen!*") or if it involves the progressive aspect in addition to the perfect aspect ("The sun *has been shining* all morning").

- **Other examples:** "Sacramento *has been* the capital of California since 1854." (present perfect)

  "We *have been driving* for hours—are you sure you know the way to Whitneyville?" (present perfect with progressive aspect)

  "Bald eagles *have* occasionally *been seen* down by Black Creek." (present perfect in passive voice)

See also: compound tense

present progressive

A red warning light on the dashboard is flashing.

The present progressive is a form of the verb that combines the present **tense** and progressive **aspect**. You use it when you're describing something that is going on right now. For instance, in the sentence above, the verb phrase "is flashing" is in the present progressive, because the event it's discussing is happening now.

You form the present progressive by combining a present-tense form of *be* such as *is* or *am* with the present participle of another verb. That other verb can be the main verb of the verb phrase, as in the example above, or it can be the auxiliary verb *being* if the verb phrase is in the passive **voice** ("We *are being kept* awake by your snoring ").

■ **Other examples:** "It *is starting* to snow."

"Why *are* you *looking* at me that way?"

"We can't run the water while the plumbing *is being fixed*." (present progressive in passive voice)

See also: compound tense

present tense

Over a billion people live in China.

The present tense is a form of the verb that you use when you're discussing something as going on now. For instance, in the sentence above, the verb *live* is in the present tense, because it's describing an event (over a billion people living in China) as something that is happening now.

■ **Other examples:** "Vladimir *knows* how to yodel."

"Electric current *consists* of quickly flowing electrons."

"Peoria, Illinois, *is surrounded* by farmland." (passive-voice construction combining the present-tense *is* with the past participle *surrounded*)

■ **Useful tip:** Not every sentence in the present tense is really discussing events in the present time. We also use the present tense for retelling the plot of stories ("The wolf *swallows* Little Red Riding Hood") and for talking about actions that have happened in the past and are almost certain to happen in the future too ("Most summers I *go* to Vermont").

See also: future tense, habitual aspect, historical present, irregular verb, past tense, present perfect, present progressive, regular verb preterite   **See** past tense

principal parts

The principal parts of a verb are the forms that you need to know in order to construct any other form of the verb. The principal parts of a verb include

- the bare infinitive (*speak*, for instance)
- the past tense (*spoke*)
- the past participle (*spoken*
- the present participle (*speaking*).

Knowing the bare infinitive will help you create present and future-tense forms ("I *speak*"; "she *speaks*"; "they *will speak*"), and knowing the participles will allow you to create forms in the passive voice ("the word *was spoken*") or the progressive or perfect aspect ("we *are speaking*"; "they *have spoken*").

- **Other examples:** *buy, bought, bought, buying*

  know, knew, known, knowing

  sing, sang, sung, singing

- **Exception:** The present-tense forms of *be* (*am, are,* and *is*) can't be constructed from the infinitive, and *be* has two different past-tense forms (*was* and *were*). So *be* doesn't really have principal parts in the same way that other verbs do.

- **Useful tip:** A dictionary entry for a bare infinitive form (*ask*, for instance) of a verb will usually list the other principal parts of the verb as well. If only two other principal parts are listed (*asked, asking*), that usually means that the past-tense form and the past-participle form are identical.

See also: irregular verb, regular verb

progressive aspect

The progressive (sometimes also called "the imperfect") is one of the possible **aspects** of a verb—that is, it's a way of describing the relation between a particular action and a particular point in time. You use the progressive aspect when you want to describe an event as going on at a particular point in time. In other words, the <u>progressive</u> aspect describes events that are (or were or will be) in <u>progress</u>.

For instance, the verb phrase "are expanding" is in the progressive aspect in the cartoon below because it expresses the idea that the expansion of the recycling program is going on at a particular point in time (right now).

You form the progressive aspect of a verb by combining a form of *be* with a present participle of the verb.

WE ARE EXPANDING THE RECYCLING PROGRAM, AND WE WILL BE PUTTING SOLAR PANELS ON CITY HALL!

Earth Day!

The mayor gives a very progressive speech.

- **Other examples:** "I *am feeling* a little queasy."

  "The sun *was setting* by the time we got to the beach."

  "Emma and Vladimir *will be playing* a kazoo duet at the spring concert."

- **Useful tip:** Since present participles can also act as adjectives, and since *be* is a linking verb, many sentences in the progressive aspect ("A light *is shining*") can also be described as being in **simple tense** and having an adjective as a **complement** to the subject ("A light is *shining*") . The same is true of passive-voice constructions, which combine the linking verb *be* with a past participle.

See also: compound tense, future progressive, past progressive, perfect aspect, present progressive

pronoun

Pronouns, such as *she, them, ourselves,* and *whom,* are one of the **parts of speech.** Pronouns stand for nouns, and they fill the same overall role in a sentence that nouns do—that is, they can act as subjects or as objects—but unlike nouns, pronouns prefer to act alone. They aren't used with articles ("*the* us"), with demonstratives ("*those* them"), or with adjective modifiers ("*expensive* it"). Since a pronoun isn't a noun itself—it only stands for a noun—it's important for the context of the sentence to make it clear what noun the pronoun refers to. That noun is called the **antecedent** of the pronoun.

- **Other examples:** "I like field hockey, but I'm not really good at *it.*" (*It* stands for *field hockey.*)

  "Of all the musk oxen in town, *yours* is the hairiest." (*Yours* stands for *your musk ox.*)

  "Nobody's chili is spicier than *ours.*" (*Ours* stands for *our chili.*)

See also: agreement, antecedent, demonstrative, indefinite pronoun, intensive pronoun, negative pronoun, objective pronoun, personal pronoun, possessive pronoun, reflexive pronoun, relative pronoun, subjective pronoun

proper adjective

A proper adjective is an adjective that refers to a specific person, place, thing, or group. Most proper adjectives are made from proper nouns. For instance, the proper adjective *American* comes from the proper noun *America.* Since proper nouns are usually capitalized, proper adjectives are too.

- **Other examples:** *Jewish* (from *Jew*)
  Asian (from *Asia*)
  Victorian (from Queen *Victoria* of Great Britain)

- **Exception:** *French* is usually capitalized because it comes from the proper noun *France,* but compound words such as *french fries* are usually written lowercase.

- **Useful tip:** Not every proper adjective comes from a proper noun—for instance, *Democratic* and *Republican* are proper adjectives when they refer to particular political parties, even though they're derived from the common nouns *democracy* and *republic,* not from proper nouns.

See also: proper noun

proper noun

This Halloween, I'm going to dress as the Statue of Liberty.

A proper noun—such as *Rosa Parks, Arizona,* or *Boston Red Sox*—is a noun that identifies a particular person, place, or thing, as opposed to common nouns like *woman, state,* or *team.* Proper nouns usually start with a capital letter, to help distinguish them from ordinary nouns.

When a title (such as *king* or *president*) is used as part of a name, it becomes part of a proper noun, so it gets capitalized: "In 1865, *President Lincoln* was assassinated." In other contexts, it's usually lowercase: "*Abraham Lincoln* was the sixteenth president." Likewise, a word like *mother* or *god* can be an ordinary noun—there are billions of mothers in the world, and many religions worship many different gods—but it can also be used as a proper noun: "Please, *Mother,* may I have another helping of cauliflower?" "Do you believe in *God?*"

 Other examples: "*Vladimir* lives on *Maple Street.*"

"*Gentron Corporation* is donating a new soccer field to *Madison Middle School.*"

See also: common noun, proper adjective

Q

question tag

A question tag is a word or set of words that you attach to the end of a sentence to turn a declarative statement into a question. For instance, you can turn the statement "I really am the smartest person in the class" into a question by attaching a question tag: "I really am the smartest person in the class, *don't you think?*" A sentence that is turned into a question by adding a question tag is called a "tag question."

 Other examples: "Today is Thursday, *isn't it?*"

"It's too bad Emma spilled soda on her prize-winning watercolor, *huh?*"

"So you think you can beat me at chess, *do you?*"

See also: declarative sentence, interrogative sentence

Is Jasmine playing or not?

question word

How far is it to the North Pole?

A question word, such as *which* or *why*, is a word that you use to ask for a specific kind of information. Not every question uses a question word. If you're wondering whether something is true or false—in other words, if you're just looking for a yes or no answer—you usually turn the sentence into a question by rearranging the word order. For instance, you would turn the statement "Gnomes are good at geometry" into the question "Are gnomes good at geometry?"

The questions that use question words are ones that can't be answered with "yes" or "no." There are three main types of question words:

1. *Who* and its objective form *whom* always act as pronouns. If a clause begins with *who*, the question word is acting as the subject of the clause, and so it's followed by the verb in the usual way: "Who wants a pretzel?" If *whom* stands for the object of the verb, it usually gets moved toward the beginning of the clause, and the subject and verb get rearranged according to the usual rule for **interrogative sentences**: "Whom did you ask to the dance?" If *whom* is the object of a preposition, the preposition can either stay where it is ("Whom did you give the package to?") or it can go at the front of the clause along with the question word: "To whom did you give the package?"

2. *What, which,* and the possessive *whose* can act either as determiners ("What size shoe do you wear?") or as pronouns ("Whose was the best answer?"). Either way, if the question word is the subject or part of the subject of the clause, the verb comes after the subject, just as it would in an ordinary sentence: "Which size fits you best?" If the question word is an object or part of an object of the verb, it usually gets placed at the beginning of the clause, and the subject and verb get rearranged according to the usual rule for interrogative sentences: "Which should I buy?"

3. *Where, when, why,* and *how* usually act as adverbs. They usually appear at the beginning of the clause, and the subject and verb are rearranged according to the usual rule for interrogative sentences: "Why can't I buy a dirt bike?" But when the question word *how* is acting as an adverb modifying an adjective or another adverb, the word it modifies gets brought to the front of the clause too: "How far is it to the North Pole?"

See also: relative pronoun, yes-no question

R

referent

I'm going to the Big Apple for New Year's Eve.

A referent is the person or thing that a particular **nominal** (that is, a word, phrase, or clause acting as a noun) actually <u>refers</u> to. For instance, if your friend tells you "I'm going to *the Big Apple* for New Year's Eve," it's likely that your friend is going to New York City, because the phrase "the Big Apple" traditionally refers to New York City. A lot of the time, you can only tell what the referent of something is if you know the context. If you meet up with your friend, and the first thing he or she says is "*That kid* is so cool," you have no way of knowing who the referent of the phrase "that kid" is—unless, of course, your friend is gesturing toward someone in particular. In writing, it's usually good to construct your sentences in such a way as to make it possible for your reader to understand the referent of each nominal. But it's sometimes OK if the referent isn't clear until afterwards—the reader doesn't always have to understand the referent right away. In fact, that can be a useful way to spark a reader's interest. For instance, you might begin a paragraph with the sentence "*A horrifying, grisly sight* greeted my eyes." The reader, who has no idea what horrifying, grisly sight you're referring to, will naturally be curious and will want to read further to find out what you saw.

See also: antecedent

reflexive pronoun

I decided to treat myself to some ice cream.

You use reflexive pronouns (such as *myself* in the example above) as grammatical **objects** when the object refers to the same person or thing as the subject. The reflexive pronouns include the personal pronouns *myself, ourselves, yourself, yourselves, himself, herself, itself,* and *themselves,* as well as the indefinite pronoun *oneself.*

- **Examples:** "Sometimes I amaze *myself.*" (direct object of the verb *amaze*) "*The senators* voted to give *themselves* a raise." (indirect object of the infinitive *to give*)
  "*Max* looked at *himself* in the mirror" (object of the preposition *at*)

- **Useful tip:** The reflexive pronouns can also be used not to fill any particular grammatical role, but simply to emphasize a noun or pronoun that has already been mentioned. One famous example of this comes from a speech by Franklin D. Roosevelt: "We have nothing to fear but *fear itself.*"

- **Caution:** Many people use reflexive pronouns as the subject of a sentence ("Edgar and *myself* went to the art museum"), or as an object even when the object is different from the subject ("Mom agreed to take Edgar and *myself* to the art museum"). These constructions may sound fancy, but they are generally considered to be incorrect. It's better to say "Edgar and *I* went to the art museum" or "Mom agreed to take Edgar and me to the art museum."

See also: intensive pronoun, subjective pronoun, reflexive pronoun

regular

In everyday English, something is "regular" if it follows a predictable rule or pattern. A regular hexagon, for instance, is a hexagon on which every side is the same length and every angle has the same measure. Similarly, in grammar, a word form is called "regular" if it follows the same pattern as most other words of the same type. For instance, if you know the usual rule for making short adjectives into comparatives, you'll be able to form the comparative of almost any short adjective you come across: *warm* becomes *warmer,* *hard* becomes *harder,* *sweet* becomes *sweeter,* *dark* becomes *darker,* and so on. These are regular comparative forms. But the comparative of *good* is *better,* and the comparative of *much* is *more.* Forms like these, which don't follow the usual rule, are called "irregular" forms.

See also: irregular plural, irregular verb, regular plural, regular verb

regular plural

Most singular nouns in English can be made plural by adding *–s* or *–es* to them. Nouns that follow this pattern are said to have regular plurals. Here are the rules for regular plurals:

- If the word ends in a consonant other than *s, x, z, sh,* or *ch,* you make it plural by just adding *–s: chicken* becomes *chickens, head* becomes *heads, planet* becomes *planets,* and so on.

- If the word ends in *s, x, z, sh,* or *ch,* you make it plural by adding *–es: bus* becomes *buses, wish* becomes *wishes, match* becomes *matches,* and so on.

- If the word ends in a *y* that's acting as a vowel, you make it plural by changing *y* to *i* and adding *–es: baby* becomes *babies, fly* becomes *flies, sky* becomes *skies,* and so on. A *y* following a vowel counts as a consonant, so the word follows rule #1: *boy* becomes *boys, day* becomes *days, ray* becomes *rays,* and so on.

- If the word ends in *a, e, i,* or *u,* you make it plural by adding *–s: flea* becomes *fleas, grove* becomes *groves, ski* becomes *skis, emu* becomes *emus,* and so on.

- If the word ends in an *o* after a consonant, you usually make it plural by adding *–es: motto* becomes *mottoes, potato* becomes *potatoes,* and so on. If the word ends in *o* following another vowel, it just gets an *–s: kazoo* becomes *kazoos, patio* becomes *patios, video* becomes *videos,* and so on.

See also: irregular plural

regular verb

Most verbs in English have very predictable forms for their past tense and past participle. For these verbs, which are called regular verbs, you can create any form of the verb—no matter what **number, person, tense, aspect,** or **voice**—if you only know the bare infinitive form—the form it appears under in the dictionary. Here are the basic rules for regular verbs:

- Most of the ordinary present-tense forms of the verb are identical to the bare infinitive: "I *walk*," "we *walk*," "you *walk*," "they *walk*."

- Third-person singular present-tense verbs are formed from the bare infinitive, usually by just adding *–s*: "he/she/it *walks*." If the infinitive ends in *s, x, z, sh,* or *ch,* you add *–es*: *rush* becomes *rushes*. If the infinitive ends in a vowel *y,* you change *y* to *i* and add *–es*: *cry* becomes *cries*. If it ends in a single *o,* you just add *–es*: *veto* becomes *vetoes*.

- The past tense and past participle are formed from the bare infinitive, usually by just adding *–ed*: *walk* becomes *walked*. If the infinitive ends in *e,* just add *–d*: *race* becomes *raced*. If the infinitive ends in a vowel *y,* change the *y* to *i* and add *–ed*: *carry* becomes *carried*.

- The present participle is formed from the bare infinitive, usually by just adding *–ing*: *walk* becomes *walking*. If the infinitive ends in a silent *e,* replace the *e* with *–ing*: *race* becomes *racing*.

See also: irregular verb, principal parts

relative clause

People who live in glass houses shouldn't throw stones.

A relative clause is a kind of **subordinate clause** that follows and modifies a noun or noun phrase. For instance, in the sentence above, the clause "who live in glass houses" is a relative clause acting as an adjective to modify *people*—it tells <u>what kind</u> of people shouldn't throw stones. (Actually, you probably shouldn't throw stones even if you live in a wood or brick house—it isn't very nice!) Relative clauses sometimes begin with the possessive adjective *whose,* but usually they begin with one of four relative pronouns: *who, whom, which,* or *that.* When the relative pronoun is a grammatical object in its relative clause, it's often OK to leave it out altogether. For example, in the sentence "The book *[that] I have to read* is 500 pages long," the relative pronoun *that* is the object of the infinitive "to read," so you can leave it out if you like.

Other examples: "The pictures, *which we took with my new camera*, are all blurry."

"My aunt is the person *for whom I was named*."

"Is that the man *whose dog bit Vladimir*?"

See also: nonrestrictive clause, restrictive clause

relative pronoun

Is this the only trick that your dog can do?

A relative pronoun is a pronoun that introduces a **relative clause**. The relative pronouns are *who, whom, which,* and *that.* When you use a relative pronoun in a sentence, its antecedent is the noun that the clause modifies. For example, in the sentence above, the antecedent of the relative pronoun *that* is the noun *trick.*

The relative pronoun can be the subject or an object of the verb in the relative clause. Or it can be an object of a preposition in the clause. In formal writing, when a relative pronoun is the object of a preposition, you put the preposition up at the front of the clause along with the relative pronoun: "I began to lose my grasp on the branch *to which* I was clinging." In colloquial English, it's OK to leave the preposition in its usual place and just put the pronoun at the front of the clause: "I began to lose my grasp on the branch *which* I was clinging to."

Caution: A relative pronoun's **case** depends on the role it plays in the relative clause, not on the case of its antecedent. It's possible for an objective relative pronoun to have a subjective antecedent ("*She whom* you invited to dinner has arrived") or for a subjective relative pronoun to have an objective antecedent ("Don't forget to invite *us, who* are your best friends").

restrictive clause

We went back to the place where we last saw Fluffy.

A restrictive clause is a **subordinate clause** that provides information about something or someone you've just mentioned. That is to say, a restrictive clause follows a noun or noun phrase and modifies it. (In the example above, the restrictive clause "where we last saw Fluffy" modifies the noun *place.*) The extra information in a restrictive clause is necessary information—if it weren't in the sentence, the rest of the sentence would leave the reader confused as to who or what you're discussing.

- **Other examples:** "In some games, the player *who gets the lowest score* wins."

"When we get home, the first thing *that I'll do* is pour myself a big glass of iced tea."

"Winter is the time of year *when the days are shortest in the Northern Hemisphere.*"

- **Useful tip:** If the information you're adding isn't all that important—if it would be possible to tell who or what the sentence is talking about even if the extra clause weren't there—then it's called a **nonrestrictive clause** and you ordinarily set it off from the rest of the sentence with commas. For instance, if you write, "Dwight D. Eisenhower *who was the thirty-fourth president of the US* was the first Republican president in twenty years" the extra information isn't really that important to the meaning of the sentence. After all, there's only one Dwight D. Eisenhower who was a president. So you would set off the extra clause with commas and write that "Dwight D. Eisenhower, *who was the thirty-fourth president of the US,* was the first Republican president in twenty years."

See also: nonrestrictive clause, relative clause

rhetorical question

A rhetorical question is a question that you don't really expect an answer to. For instance, if you ask your sister whether she'd like a piece of blue-

Actually, it's more a suggestion than a question.

berry pie and she replies, "Hey, why not?" she most likely doesn't want you to answer her question—she just wants you to give her a piece of the pie.

- **Other examples:** "Who can forget that fateful night in 1962 when the pigs escaped?"

  "Do I <u>look</u> like I'm joking? Get back to work!"

  "When will you ever learn that jellyfish don't make good pets?"

- **Useful tip:** The set of techniques people use to make their language interesting (or impressive or beautiful or persuasive) is called "rhetoric." As you might guess, rhetorical questions are called "rhetorical" because they're a kind of rhetoric.

root

A root is a word or a part of a word that you form other words from by adding prefixes or suffixes or by combining it with another root. For instance, from the root *heat* you can make the verb *reheat* by adding the prefix *re–*, or you can make the noun *heater* by adding the suffix *–er*.

Many roots aren't actual words in English—instead, they're borrowed from words in other languages. The English words *inspect, spectator,* and *spectrum* all share the root *–spect–*, which isn't a word in English but comes from the Latin verb *specere*, which means "to look at." It's a good idea to learn to recognize the most common roots, because they'll often help you to figure out the meaning of words you've never seen before. For instance, you probably already know that *–ology* means "the study of" in words like *biology, geology,* and *zoology.* You may also know that *–hydr–* means "water" in words like "dehydrate," "hydrant," and "hydro-electric." Putting these two roots together, you can guess that *hydrology* is the study of water.

- **Useful tip:** Most good dictionaries include information about the etymology of words—that is, how the word was created over time out of prefixes, suffixes, and roots from various languages. In some cases, we can trace the etymology of a word back thousands of years to a root in a language that nobody speaks any more, such as Proto-Indo-European—the ancient language that eventually developed into modern languages like English, German, French, Spanish, Greek, Russian, Persian, and Hindi.

See also: stem

run-on sentence

The term "run-on sentence" has several different meanings:

- A lot of people use it to refer to a sentence that has a **comma splice** ("The band came to the end of the song, the audience clapped loudly")

- Other people use it to refer to a **fused sentence** ("Take the brownies out of the oven they'll burn otherwise")

- Still other people use it to refer to a sentence in which two or more clauses are connected with conjunctions such as *and* or *but* without any commas before the conjunctions ("Seals sometimes crawl up onto the shore but manatees always stay in the water"). You can fix this kind of run-on sentence by simply adding commas as needed between the clauses.

- Lastly, many people use the term to refer to a sentence that just contains too many clauses that aren't closely related to one another ("Vladimir's mother was born on the seventeenth of March, but I don't know what year, and Vladimir doesn't like pickles, because he ate too many of them when he was five years old, and five out of six people prefer the smell of freshly-mowed grass to the sound of bagpipes, but anyway why is it that a cup of heavy cream weighs less than a cup of light cream?"). A sentence like this may be perfectly grammatical, and it may be perfectly punctuated, but no reader wants to wade through such a jumble of ideas in a single sentence. You'd be better off putting the different ideas into different sentences or even different paragraphs.

See also: compound sentence, coordinating conjunction, subordinating conjunction

S

second person

The second person is the category of grammatical forms that you use when you're speaking or writing directly to someone. The only parts of speech that have second-person forms are pronouns, possessive adjectives, and verbs:

- The second-person pronouns are *you, yourself,* and *yours.*

- The second-person possessive adjective is *your.*

- Except for the word *be,* second-person verbs in the present tense are identical to the bare infinitive form of the verb, and in the past tense they're identical to the ordinary past tense of the verb. (For the verb *be,* see the chart at the entry for **conjugate**.)

Useful tip: The second person also is useful for discussing general situations and facts that don't have anything to do with the person you're addressing ("In order to be crowned king of England, *you* have to have been born into the royal family"). You can even use it to refer to yourself in a way that invites the reader or listener to imagine being in your situation ("I find that people tend to laugh in *your* face when *you* tell them *your* name is Edgar Babbitt Throcksnorkle IV").

See also: agreement, first person, third person

sentence

Warthogs exist.

A sentence is a set of words that follows the rules of grammar and expresses some idea about what something (or someone) is or does (or was, or did, or will be, etc.). Every complete sentence contains at least one **independent clause**, which means every complete sentence has a **subject** and a **predicate** containing a **finite verb**. Written sentences start with a capital letter, and they end with a period, a question mark, or an exclamation point, depending on whether they're making a statement, asking a question, or expressing an emotion.

Examples: "Warthogs exist."
"What did you see at the museum?"
"Next time, before you turn on the food processor, fasten the lid properly!"

See also: complex sentence, compound sentence, declarative sentence, exclamatory sentence, interrogative sentence, simple sentence

sentence adverb **See** absolute construction

sentence fragment **See** fragment

simple sentence

A simple sentence is a sentence that consists of just one clause—a subject and a predicate. For example, the simple sentence "My father's running shoes smell awful" consists of the subject "My father's running shoes" and the predicate "smell awful."

A simple sentence can be complicated, but it can't be complex.

- **Other examples:** "I'll see you tomorrow."

   "Basketballs and soccer balls are spherical."

   "The first permanent English colony in North America was established in Jamestown, Virginia."

- **Useful tip:** Simple sentences are only called "simple" because they consist of a single clause. They can actually be pretty complicated, using difficult words and consisting of a lot of different grammatical parts—like the sentence in the cartoon above—as long as they still have just one subject, one predicate, and no subordinate clauses.

See also: complex sentence, compound sentence, compound-complex sentence

simple subject

The paint on those chairs hasn't dried yet.

The simple subject of a clause is the noun, pronoun, or other nominal that the subject of the sentence is built up around—that is, it's the **head** of the noun phrase that's acting as the subject. For instance, in the sentence above, the subject is "The paint on those chairs," but the simple subject is the noun *paint*—the other words in the subject (the article *the* and the prepositional phrase "on those chairs") are just adding information about the paint.

When you're trying to figure out whether to use a singular or plural verb, look at the simple subject of the clause—if it's a singular word, the verb should be singular too, and if it's a plural word, the verb should be plural, regardless of what other singular or plural nouns appear in the whole subject.

- **Other examples:** "The _smallest_ of the three islands is named Parrot Cay."

  "_Answering_ the questions on the test was pretty easy."

  "The _knowledge_ that I played as well as I could despite my sprained ankle makes losing the game a little less disappointing."

See also: compound subject

simple tense

He counted the chocolate chips.

A verb form is said to be in a simple tense if it has no particular **aspect.** Simple tense only tells whether the sentence takes place in the past, present, or future; unlike a **compound tense**, it describes events as simply happening rather than as being finished or still going on at the point in time the sentence is talking about. For example, the past-tense sentence above is in a simple tense, but the sentences "He *had counted* the chocolate chips," "He *was counting* the chocolate chips," and "He *had been counting* the chocolate chips" aren't.

- **Other examples:** "When the earthquake *struck*, the bridge *collapsed*."

  "I *dislike* dressing up for parties."

  "Finishing this assignment *will take* at least an hour."

See also: future tense, past tense, perfect aspect, present tense, progressive aspect

singular

Words that refer to a single person, thing, or idea are said to be singular in **number.** Several different parts of speech can be singular:

- Nouns are the most obvious example. The nouns *glove, leopard, organization,* and *window,* for example, are all singular.

- Verbs take a singular form whenever their grammatical subject is singular. Much of the time, the singular form is identical to the plural form ("Emma *went* to the dance competition. Grace and Sonia *went* with her"). But third-person verbs in the present tense have different singular and plural forms ("She *goes* to a lot of dance events. The other girls only *go* once in a while").

- Pronouns take a singular form whenever they stand for a singular antecedent ("The *dance competition* usually takes place in Whitneyville, but this year *it* happened in San Rafael").

- Possessive adjectives take a singular form whenever the noun or pronoun they're formed from (<u>not</u> the noun they modify!) is singular ("The *music's* rhythms [*not* "the *musics'* rhythms"!] make it hard for anyone to sit still").

- Demonstratives take a singular form whenever they refer to a singular noun ("*That* tall *dancer* with the red hair is fantastic!").

See also: agreement, plural

split infinitive

Could you ask him to not make that annoying noise?

A split infinitive is a construction that uses an infinitive, such as "to make," but with other words (typically adverbs) stuck in between the *to* and the bare infinitive—as the *not* is in the example sentence above.

Many people—including some English teachers—consider split infinitives to be a kind of error. This is because a few hundred years ago Latin was the language that all educated Europeans studied in school. Grammar experts back then decided that the English language should work pretty much the way Latin works—and in Latin, infinitives are written as a single word. (The word *amare,* for instance, means "to love" in Latin.) So the experts came up with the rule that adverbs should go before or after the infinitive in English, but not in the middle of it. But good writers throughout the history of English have used split infinitives, and most grammar experts nowadays consider them to be perfectly OK. They're certainly fine in everyday speech or in informal writing, but you might want to ask your teacher whether he or she prefers that you avoid split infinitives in your schoolwork.

■ **Other examples:** "Don't forget *to first preheat* the oven." (could be rephrased as "to preheat the oven first")

"Do you plan *to just sit* there doing nothing all day?" (could be rephrased as "just to sit there")

"I want you to *really try your* hardest" (could be rephrased as "really to try")

See also: split verb

split verb

Vladimir has definitely proven that he has no fear of snakes.

A split verb is a verb phrase whose main verb is separated from one or more of its auxiliary verbs by one or more adverbs. For instance, the example sentence above has a split verb, because the adverb *definitely* falls between the main verb *proven* and its auxiliary *has*. Unlike **split infinitives**, split verbs are almost never considered to be a grammatical error.

■ **Other examples:** "I *have never been* to Bulgaria."

"From the top floor of the Seaview Hotel you *can almost see* the ocean."

"If you run that fast in next week's race, you *will most likely beat* all your opponents."

stem

The stem of a word is the part of the word that forms the basis for its various different **inflections**. For instance, the verb stem *walk* appears in all the various inflected forms of the verb: *walk, walks, walked, walking.* For most verbs, all the different tense forms are based on the same stem, but there are a few verbs (like *be* and *go*) that use very different stems for different forms. Likewise, all the different forms of a noun usually come from the same stem (one common exception to this is *people,* the everyday plural of *person*). Other kinds of words, such as adjectives, adverbs, and pronouns, also form inflections by adding suffixes to stems.

- **Other examples:** *shak–* in *shake, shakes, shook, shaken, shaking*

  Latin– in *Latina, Latino, Latinas, Latinos, Latina's, Latino's, Latinas', Latinos'*

  wet– in *wet, wetter, wettest*

- **Useful tip:** You'll notice that some words' stems change their spelling when the word gets inflected, even though there's no change in pronunciation—for instance, the *y* in *deny* is changed to *ie* in *denies*. Other stems change both their spelling and pronunciation (*mouse* changes to *mice*), or they change their pronunciation but not their spelling (the long *i* in the *rid–* stem of *ride* becomes a short *i* in *ridden*).

See also: root

strong verb   **See** irregular verb

subject

Only one of the two girls successfully jumped the mud puddle.

The subject of a clause is the part of the clause that tells who or what is doing the action that the verb describes. The subject can be a single noun or pronoun, as in the sentences "*Skunks* smell awful" or "*We* live in an apartment building." Or it can be a longer noun phrase, like the phrase "Only one of the two girls" in the example sentence above. Every complete clause contains a subject as well as a **predicate**, and since every complete sentence contains at least one clause, every sentence has at least one subject too.

- **Other examples:** "Suddenly a *tornado* appeared out of nowhere."

  "*A mysterious scratching and scuttling sound* came from inside the wall."

  "*To be good at chess* requires both imagination and concentration."

- **Exception:** Imperative sentences often don't actually name their subject, since the subject is usually the person you're giving orders to or requesting something from. Instead of saying "You give me that pencil, please!" it's fine to say just "Give me that pencil, please!" In sentences like this, the subject is said to be "understood."

See also: anticipatory subject, compound subject, object, simple subject, subject complement, subjective pronoun

subject complement

That stack of dishes looks unstable.

A subject complement is a word or phrase that follows a **linking verb**, describing what the subject of the verb is, becomes, or seems to be. A subject complement can be a noun, an adjective, or a longer phrase acting as a noun or adjective. For instance, in the example sentence above, the adjective *unstable* is a subject complement, because it describes the subject ("that stack of dishes").

- **Other examples:** "Tuesday is *my least favorite day of the week.*"

  "All frogs once *were tadpoles.*"

  "You sound *a little tired.*"

- **Useful tip:** Subject complements don't only appear after actual verbs. They can also follow **verbals**—words such as participles and infinitives that are derived from verbs but don't act as verbs in the grammar of the sentence. For instance, the complement "an entirely honest person" is attached to the participle *being* in the sentence "Being *an entirely honest person*, Vladimir would never claim to have seen a rhinoceros in the backyard if in fact he hadn't."

See also: linking verb, object complement

subjective pronoun

She dropped the jar of pickles on the kitchen floor.

A subjective pronoun is a pronoun that you use as a grammatical **subject**. For example, in the sentence above, *she* is a subjective pronoun because *she* is the one who dropped the jar. The subjective pronouns include the personal pronouns *I, we, you, he, she, it,* and *they,* along with the relative pronouns and question words *who* and *whoever.*

- **Other examples:** "*She* looks familiar to me."

  "Whales have to surface from time to time because *they* have lungs, not gills."

  "*Whoever* invented the thermos must have really liked hot drinks."

- **Caution:** Lots of people don't know whether to use the subjective *who* or the objective *whom* in questions such as "Who[m] should I say is calling?" or "Who[m] do you think we should invite?" To decide which to use, try turning the question into a statement and replacing *who* or *whom* with the subjective *he* (or *she*) or the objective *him* (or *her*). Since "I say *he* is calling" makes more sense than "I say *him* is calling," you should use the subjective *who* when you phrase the first sentence as a question: "Who should I say is calling?" Likewise, since "You think we should invite *her*" makes more sense than "You think we should invite *she*," you know you should use the objective *whom* when you put the second sentence into question form: "Whom do you think we should invite?"

See also: objective pronoun, reflexive pronoun

subjunctive

The customer demanded that the manager give her a refund.

The subjunctive is one of the less common grammatical **moods** in English; it's the sentence form you use when you're discussing the way things could be or should be, as opposed to simply making a statement or asking a question about the way things are or were or will be. For instance, in the example above, the clause "that the manager give her a refund" is in the subjunctive mood—it describes an event (the giving of the refund) that may or may not actually happen, though the customer believes very strongly that it should.

Just like with the other moods, if you're trying to decide whether a sentence is in the subjunctive, you look at its verb forms. The subjunctive most often appears in three different constructions:

1. Noun clauses describing a situation that may or may not actually be the case. In this situation, the verb doesn't get an ordinary inflection; instead it's replaced with the **bare infinitive**—the form in which the verb would be entered in a dictionary. For example, in the sentence "It's important *that each student have the opportunity to speak*," the verb in the noun clause is the subjunctive *have* (the bare infinitive) and not the indicative *has* (as you would normally expect for a third-person singular subject).

2. Noun clauses that are direct objects of *wish*. In this situation, the verb goes in the past tense even if you're discussing the present moment: "I wish I *had seventeen billion dollars*." If the verb in the noun clause is a form of *be*, traditional rules say that the subjunctive should be *were*, even in the first-person singular ("I wish I *were six feet tall*") and third-person singular ("I wish *my brother were here*"). In everyday speech, however, many people use *was* as a first-person and third-person singular subjunctive ("I wish *my brother was here*").

3. **Subjunctive conditional** sentences. These are sentences that discuss what would happen if things were different than they are. See the following entry for a detailed explanation.

See also: imperative, indicative

subjunctive conditional

Subjunctive conditional verb forms are used in **conditional** sentences to describe things that are extremely unlikely or that aren't actually the case. In a sentence like "If we had a spare inner tube, we could fix this in five minutes," both the subordinate clause ("If we *had* a spare inner tube") and the independent clause ("we *could* fix this in five minutes") use subjunctive conditional forms.

Subjunctive conditional verbs look like past-tense forms, even when they refer to present or future events. The subjunctive conditional form of *be* is always *were,* even in cases like the first-person singular where the ordinary past tense is *was.* In conditional sentences that use the subjunctive, the subordinate clause is written with a subjunctive conditional verb (like *had*) and the independent clause is written with a subjunctive conditional **modal verb** (like *could* in the verb phrase "could fix").

The subjunctive conditional outlook on life. . .

■ **Other examples:** "If the world *were* flat, it *would* be impossible to sail around it."

"*Would* you still like me if I *were* less cute?"

"If I *knew* the answer, I *might* tell you."

■ **Useful tip:** Future-tense subjunctive conditional verbs often take the form of *were* plus an infinitive in the subordinate clause of the sentence ("If you *were to stay* here all day, you'd see a lot of people walk by"). Past-tense subjunctive conditional verbs look like past perfect verbs when they appear in subordinate clauses, and they look like present perfect verbs when they come after the modal verb in their independent clauses ("If you *had told* me earlier, I could *have arrived* on time").

See also: conditional conjunction, indicative, subjunctive

subordinate clause

When I saw the smoke pouring out of the kitchen, I knew I was in trouble.

A subordinate clause is a **clause** that can't stand alone as a sentence—it has to be connected somehow to an independent clause. For instance, in the sentence above, the subordinate clause ("When I saw the smoke pouring out of the kitchen") is obviously incomplete—it needs to be connected to the independent clause ("I knew I was in trouble") in order to make a full sentence. In comparison, the independent clause could be a sentence all by itself.

A subordinate clause can come before its independent clause or after it, or it can even be **embedded** in the middle of the independent clause.

■ **Other examples:** "*Though it sounds exciting*, I prefer not to float over Niagara Falls in a barrel."

"I only told my secret to Vladimir—*who then told everyone else in town.*"

"The town *where we stopped for the night* calls itself the popcorn capital of the world."

See also: adverbial clause, complex sentence, nonrestrictive clause, noun clause, relative clause, restrictive clause, subordinating conjunction

subordinating conjunction

If you're squeamish, you shouldn't visit the sausage factory.

Like all **conjunctions**, a subordinating conjunction is a word that helps to connect one part of a sentence to another. For instance, in the sentence above, the subordinating conjunction *if* helps to clarify how one idea ("you're squeamish") is connected to another ("you shouldn't visit the sausage factory"). A clause that begins with a subordinating conjunction is a subordinate clause; when you come across it, you know there must be an independent clause somewhere around for the subordinate clause to be connected to. Some of the most common subordinating conjunctions are *although, because, if, unless, until, when,* and *while.*

■ **Other examples:** "You're welcome to mow the lawn *while* I nap in the hammock."

"*Unless* my eyes deceive me, Emma has a new haircut."

"I hate playing football with you *because* you always argue over the rules."

See also: coordinating conjunction, correlative conjunction

suffix

You'll never be happy if all you care about is your own happiness.

A suffix consists of one or more syllables that you attach to the end of a word (or to a **root** or **stem**) to produce a new word with a different meaning. For instance, in the sentence above, the noun *happiness* is formed by adding the suffix *–ness* to the adjective *happy.* (In the process, of course, the *y* of *happy* changes to an *i*.) As this example shows, adding a suffix to a word can produce a new word that belongs to a different part of speech.

■ **Other examples:** *–ful* as in *hopeful* or *truthful*
–or as in *actor* or *collector*
–ize as in *fossilize* or *hospitalize*

■ **Useful tip:** Most dictionaries don't bother to define every possible word that can be formed by adding suffixes to other words. Instead, an entry for a shorter word will often end with a list of the longer words that can be derived from it by adding suffixes. For instance, the entry for *quaint* might end by listing the adverb *quaintly* and the noun *quaintness*, leaving you (the clever reader) to figure out what these words mean based on the meaning of the original word and the meanings of the suffixes.

See also: affix, prefix

superlative degree

The superlative degree is a way of using an adjective or adverb to describe something as having more of some quality than any other similar thing. For example, in the cartoon dialogue on the next page, *tastiest* is the superlative degree of the adjective *tasty*—it makes it clear that the pie in question had more tastiness than any other octopus pie. For most short adjectives you form the superlative by adding *–est*. For instance, *deep* becomes *deepest*. But there are some special spelling rules:

- If the adjective ends in a single vowel and a single consonant, you usually double the consonant before adding *–est*: *wet* becomes *wettest*.
- If the adjective ends in an *e*, you usually form the superlative by just adding *–st*: *blue* becomes *bluest*.
- If the adjective ends in *y* you form the superlative by replacing the *y* with *–iest*: *tiny* becomes *tiniest*.

For longer adjectives and most adverbs, you form the superlative by simply modifying the word with *most*: "Getting a standing ovation for my performance as Juliet was the *most memorable* experience of my life."

Sometimes the superlative degree isn't all that impressive.

- **Exception:** The adjectives *good* and *bad* have unusual superlative forms. Rather than "goodest" and "baddest," the superlatives are *best* and *worst*. Likewise, the superlative of the adverb *well* is also *best*. The superlative of the adverb *badly* can be either *worst* or *most badly*.

- **Caution:** Not all adjectives and adverbs have a superlative degree form. Some, like the adjective *only* and the adverb *once,* can only be used in the positive degree. Many people—including some English teachers— feel that the word *unique* works this way too, and that it's a mistake to talk about something being "more unique" or "the most unique."

See also: comparative degree, periphrastic, positive degree

syntax

This how understand supposed anyone is to?

Syntax is a term for the way words are put together to form phrases and sentences. Every language has its own rules of syntax, which not only determine what is and what isn't a grammatical sentence but also make it possible for people to understand each other when they speak or write. For instance, the rules of English syntax ordinarily require that the grammatical subject come before the verb and that grammatical objects (if there are any) come after the verb. If we didn't have such a rule, a sentence like "The player hit the ball with great force" would mean exactly the same thing as "The ball hit the player with great force"—which would make communicating very difficult!

T

tag question   See question tag

tense

I hated candied yams the first time I tried them, I hate them now, and I always will hate them!

The tense of a verb is a way of describing how the verb's form tells when in time a particular action happens. Every verb or verb phrase has a tense, which tells whether the action of the verb takes place in the past, present, or future. (In the sentence above, you can see all three tenses at work.) You signal the tense of a verb either by making changes to the verb itself or by adding auxiliary verbs such as *will* and *shall*.

■ **Other examples:** "My sister *attended* Wakashaw High School." (past tense)

"My sister *attends* Wakashaw High School." (present tense)

"My sister *will attend* Wakashaw High School." (future tense)

See also: aspect, compound tense, future tense, past tense, present tense, simple tense

third person

The third person is the category of grammatical forms that you use to discuss people or things other than yourself and whoever you're speaking or writing to. The only parts of speech that have third-person forms are pronouns, possessive adjectives, and verbs:

- The third-person pronouns are *he, him, himself, his; she, her, herself, hers; it, itself;* and *they, them, themselves,* and *theirs.*

- The third-person possessive adjectives are *his, her, its,* and *their.*

- In the present tense, most third-person plural verbs are identical to the bare infinitive form of the verb, while third-person singular verbs are usually formed by adding *–s* to the bare infinitive. Past-tense third-person verbs are usually identical to the simple past-tense form. (For the verb *be,* see the chart at the entry for **conjugate**.)

See also: agreement, first person, third person

transitive verb

The steamroller accidentally flat-
tened a parked car.

A transitive verb is a verb that has a **direct object**. For example, in the sentence above, the verb *flattened* is transitive, because there's something that's being flattened ("a parked car").

Most English verbs can take direct objects, although there are a few—such as *snore* and *kneel*—that never do, at least in ordinary usage. But many verbs can be either transitive or intransitive depending on the particular sentence they're used in. For instance, the verb *stop* is transitive in a sentence such as "Local activists tried to *stop* the construction of the new highway," where it takes a direct object ("the construction of the new highway"), but not in a sentence like "Does this bus *stop* at the mall?"

- **Other examples:** "I *loathe* accordion music."

  "When the tornado *reached* the town, it *destroyed* several houses and *uprooted* dozens of trees."

  "Jasmine will *design* the sets and costumes for the play."

- **Useful tip:** Linking verbs such as *be* or *seem* may seem to take direct objects, but they actually take **subject complements**.

- **Useful tip:** Children's dictionaries often don't tell you whether a verb is transitive or intransitive, but student dictionaries and adult dictionaries usually do, by using abbreviations such as *tr. v.* and *intr. v.* (or *v.t.* and *v.i.*) before the definitions.

See also: complex transitive verb, intransitive verb

U

understood

Riding horses may not sound like fun to you, but it does to me.

In the sentence above, the second clause is incomplete—the auxiliary verb *does* isn't connected to any main verb. But the meaning of the clause is obvious—it's really saying something like "but it does sound like fun to me." The reader has no trouble making sense of the sentence because the first clause contains the words that are missing in the second. In a situation like this, where some important words are left out but the meaning of the sentence is clear anyway, the missing words are said to be "understood."

- **Other examples:** "[*You*] Make me a grilled-cheese sandwich, please."

   "[*It's a*] Good thing I found you in time!"

   "I looked at her, and she [*looked*] at me."

V

verb

Next time, I suggest you try the jeans on before you buy them.

Verbs, such as *suggest, try,* and *buy* in the sentence above, are one of the **parts of speech**. They're words that describe someone (or something) as doing something, experiencing something, or being a particular way. In

English grammar, verbs are crucial—you can't have a complete sentence without one.

Verbs can be used singly, or they can be built into a verb phrase with one main verb and one or more special verbs called **auxiliary verbs**. In every sentence, the verb or verbs can take various forms (called **inflections**) that help to communicate information such as

- when something happened (**tense**)
- whether it's still going on (**aspect**)
- whether it's being done by one person or several (**number**)
- whether somebody is doing something or having something done to them (**voice**).

■ **Other examples:** "Max *forgot* his lunch again."

"We *have been waiting* for hours."

"I *will* never *forget* the heroic way you *confronted* that angry squirrel."

■ **Caution:** Not everything that looks like a verb really is one! There are some words (called **verbals**) that are derived from verbs and look like verbs, but they don't actually act as verbs; instead, they act as nouns, adjectives, or adverbs. For instance, the word "locked" in the phrase "a locked door" looks like a past-tense verb, but it's actually an adjective describing the door.

See also: action verb, clause, finite verb, intransitive verb, irregular verb, linking verb, mood, phrasal verb, regular verb, transitive verb, verb phrase

verbal

The landowner, annoyed, directed our attention to the large "NO TRESPASSING" sign on a nearby fence post.

How many verbs are there in the sentence above? Three of the words look like they could be verbs—*annoyed, directed*, and *trespassing*—but only one of them (*directed*) is acting as a verb in the grammar of the sentence. The others are filling other roles: *annoyed* is acting as an adjective that describes the landowner, while *trespassing* is acting as a noun, naming an action. These words, which are derived from verbs but don't act grammatically as verbs, are called verbals.

See also: gerund, infinitive, participle, verbal adjective, verbal noun

verbal adjective

In the cartoon below, the words *annoying* and *annoyed* are not verbs but **verbals**—they're derived from verbs, but they don't act as verbs in the grammar of the sentence. In this case, they act as adjectives describing the nonexistent *flies* and the very real *hornet*, so they're known (as you might guess) as verbal adjectives. There are two kinds of verbal adjectives:

1. A verbal adjective is made from the present participle (the –*ing* form) of the verb when the noun it describes is <u>doing</u> the action in question. For instance, in the cartoon, the flies are (Vlad thinks) doing the annoying, so the verbal adjective uses the present participle of *annoy*.

2. A verbal adjective is made from the past participle of the verb when the noun it describes is <u>undergoing</u> the action in question. For instance, in the cartoon, the hornet is experiencing annoyance, so the verbal adjective uses the past participle of *annoy*.

Watch out for those pesky verbal adjectives!

See also: participial phrase, past participle, present participle, verbal noun

verbal noun

Babies learn to talk by imitating the sounds grown-ups make.

In the sentence above, the words *talk* and *imitating* are not verbs but **verbals**—they're derived from verbs, but they don't act as verbs in the grammar of the sentence. In this case, they act as nouns, naming the act of talking and the act of imitating, so they're known (as you might guess) as verbal nouns. A verbal noun can fill any role an ordinary noun can fill—it can act as a subject, an object, or a complement. There are two kinds of verbal nouns:

1. A verbal noun can be made from the infinitive form of the verb— usually together with the preposition *to*. For example, in the sentence above, the infinitive *to talk* acts as the direct object of the verb *learn*— it names the thing that babies learn.

2. A verbal noun can be made from the present participle (the *–ing* form) of the verb. For example, in the sentence above, the present participle *imitating* acts as the object of the preposition *by*—it names the method that babies use in learning to talk.

See also: gerund, infinitive, verbal adjective

verb phrase

> *If your birthday isn't February 29th, I must have been thinking of someone else.*

The sentence above has two clauses. The first clause has just one verb (the *is* in the contraction *isn't*). But the second clause has four verbs, all in a row: *must have been thinking.* These verbs act together as a verb phrase—a **main verb** (*thinking,* in this case) with three **auxiliary verbs** that help to express the meaning of the verb.

The verbs in a verb phrase don't always appear immediately next to each other. Sometimes an adverb or an adverbial phrase comes between them: "You *could* at the very least *have taken* your muddy boots off before you came into the house." And in questions, the grammatical subject often falls between the first auxiliary verb and the rest of the verbs in the verb phrase: "*Will* the universe *expand* forever?"

Though most verb phrases have only one main verb, it's possible for the auxiliary verbs in a verb phrase to be connected to two or more verbs at once. For instance, in the sentence "Vladimir is very talented—he *can sing, dance,* and *tell* funny jokes," the auxiliary verb *can* applies to all three main verbs (*sing, dance,* and *tell*).

voice

As Max walked innocently down the street, suddenly his pant leg was attacked by a tiny puppy.

The sentence above uses verbs in two very different ways, based on whether the grammatical subject of the verb is also the **agent**—the one responsible for the action or event the verb describes:

1. In the first clause of the sentence, Max is the grammatical subject, and he himself is also the one who's doing the action (walking). This is the way most sentences in English work.

2. The second clause works differently. The pant leg is the grammatical subject, but it isn't doing the attacking—instead, it's undergoing the attacking, and the one's who's attacking (the puppy) appears only in a prepositional phrase tacked on to the end of the clause.

These two ways of using verbs are called voices. Every verb form in English uses one or the other of these voices. Clauses whose subject is also the agent are in the **active voice**, and clauses whose subject is not the agent are in the **passive voice**.

See also: aspect, mood

W

weak verb **See** regular verb

Y

yes-no question

Though many questions begin with **question words** like *which* or *when*, not all of them do. Some, like the tricky question Emma asks in the dialogue on the next page, simply start with a form of the verb *be* or with an auxiliary verb, followed by the grammatical subject. This is the kind of question you use when you're not looking for a particular kind of information—when you just want to know whether some statement is true or not. Since the answer is usually either yes or no, this kind of question is called a "yes-no question."

It seemed like a simple yes-no question.

- **Other examples:** "*Can* antelopes outrun leopards?"

  "*Are* those your socks?"

  "*Did* Confucius live before or after Muhammad?"

- **Useful tip:** In everyday life we often answer yes-no questions with an answer other than a simple yes or no. Possible answers to yes-no questions include "Maybe," "Definitely!" "I don't know," "Why do you want to know?" and "Only if you promise not to tell Martha."

See also: interrogative sentence, operator

Z

zero article

It's the usual story—boy meets girl, boy loses girl, and so on. . . .

Most of the time singular nouns have to have a definite article or some other kind of **determiner** attached to them when they appear in a sentence. But some nouns are usually used without determiners:

- proper nouns referring to a one-of-a-kind things (like *Tokyo* or *Romeo and Juliet*)

- nouns that refer not to an object but to a substance, phenomenon, or a mass or collection of things (like *water, electricity,* or *furniture*)

- nouns that refer to some very general concept (like *truth* or *happiness*).

But what about the example sentence on the previous page? Why isn't it "*a* boy meets *a* girl" or "*the* boy meets *the* girl" or some such phrasing? This grammatical construction without a determiner is known as "zero article," and though it may seem to break the rules of English, good writers do use zero article from time to time, especially when they want to describe things as being examples of very general categories, rather than calling attention to them as specific individual things.

Other examples: "You've just got to take *pen* in hand and write."

"We could hear the roar of the crowd and the crack of *bat* against *ball.*"

"He devoured *sandwich* after *sandwich* without stopping."

See also: abstract noun, concrete noun

How to Pronounce Grammar Terms:

absolute ăb′sə-lōot′

abstract ăb′străkt′

action ăk′shən

active ăk′tĭv

adjectival ăj′ĭk-tī′vəl

adjective ăj′ĭk-tĭv

adverb ăd′vûrb

adverbial ăd-vûr′bē-əl

affix ăf′ĭks′

agent ā′jənt

agreement ə-grē′mənt

antecedent ăn′tĭ-sēd′nt

anticipatory ăn-tĭs′ə-pə-tôr′ē

appositive ə-pŏz′ĭ-tĭv

article är′tĭ-kəl

aspect ăs′pĕkt

attributive ə-trĭb′yə-tĭv

auxiliary ôg-zĭl′yə-rē

bare bâr

cardinal kär′dn-əl

case kās

clause klôz

collective kə-lĕk′tĭv

colloquial kə-lō′kwē-əl

comma kŏm′ə

common kŏm′ən

comparative kəm-păr′ə-tĭv

complement kŏm′plə-mənt

complex kəm-plĕks′

compound kŏm′pound′

concrete kŏn′krēt′

conditional kən-dĭsh′ə-nəl

conjugate kŏn′jə-gāt′

conjunction kən-jŭngk′shən

conjunctive kən-jŭngk′tĭv

construction kən-strŭk′shən

content kŏn′tĕnt′

continuous kən-tĭn′yōō-əs

contraction kən-trăk′shən

coordinate kō-ôr′dn-ĭt

coordinating kō-ôr′dn-ā′tĭng

coordination kō-ôr′dn-ā′shən

correlative kə-rĕl′ə-tĭv

count kount

dangling dăng′glĭng

declarative dĭ-klâr′ə-tĭv

definite dĕf′ə-nĭt

degree dĭ-grē′

demonstrative dĭ-mŏn′strə-tĭv

dependent dĭ-pĕn′dənt

determiner dĭ-tûr′mə-nər

diminutive dĭ-mĭn′yə-tĭv

direct dĭ-rĕkt′

discourse dĭs′kôrs′

double dŭb′əl

ellipsis ĭ-lĭp′sĭs

elliptical ĭ-lĭp′tĭ-kəl

embedding ĕm-bĕd′ĭng

emphatic ĕm-făt′ĭk

exclamatory ĭk-sklăm′ə-tôr′ē

expression ĭk-sprĕsh′ən

factitive făk′tĭ-tĭv

feminine fĕm′ə-nĭn

finite fī′nīt′

first fûrst

fragment frăg′mənt

function fŭngk′shən

fused fyōōzd

future fyōō′chər

gender jĕn′dər

genitive jĕn′ĭ-tĭv

gerund jĕr′ənd

habitual hə-bĭch′ōō-əl

head hĕd

helping hĕl′pĭng

hierarchy hī′ə-rär′kē

historical hĭ-stôr′ĭ-kəl

idiom ĭd′ē-əm

imperative ĭm-pĕr′ə-tĭv

imperfect ĭm-pûr′fĭkt

indefinite ĭn-dĕf′ə-nĭt

independent ĭn′dĭ-pĕn′dənt

indicative ĭn-dĭk′ə-tĭv

indirect ĭn′dĭ-rĕkt′

infinitive ĭn-fĭn′ĭ-tĭv

inflection ĭn-flĕk′shən

intensifier ĭn-tĕn′sə-fī′ər

intensive ĭn-tĕn′sĭv

interjection ĭn′tər-jĕk′shən

interrogation ĭn-tĕr′ə-gā′shŭn

interrogative ĭn′tə-rŏg′ə-tĭv

intransitive ĭn-trăn′zĭ-tĭv

inversion ĭn-vûr′zhən

irregular ĭ-rĕg′yə-lər

joint joint

lexical lĕk′sĭ-kəl

linking lĭng′kĭng

logical lŏj′ĭ-kəl

main mān

masculine măs′kyə-lĭn

mass măs

modal mōd′l

modifier mŏd′ə-fī′ər

mood mōōd

negative nĕg′ə-tĭv

neuter nōō′tər

nominal nŏm′ə-nəl

nominative nŏm′ə-nə-tĭv

noncount nŏn′kount′

nonrestrictive nŏn′rĭ-strĭk′tĭv

noun noun

number nŭm′bər

object ŏb′jĕkt′

objective əb-jĕk′tĭv

operator ŏp′ə-rā′tər

ordinal ôr′dn-əl

parallel păr′ə-lĕl′

parenthetical păr′ən-thĕt′ĭ-kəl

parse pärs

part pärt

participial pär′tĭ-sĭp′ē-əl

participle pär′tĭ-sĭp′əl

particle pär′tĭ-kəl

passive păs′ĭv

past păst

perfect pûr′fĭkt

periodic pîr′ē-ŏd′ĭk

periphrastic pĕr′ə-frăs′tĭk

person pûr′sən

personal pûr′sə-nəl

phrasal frā′zəl

phrase frāz

pluperfect plōō-pûr′fĭkt

plural plōōr′əl

positive pŏz′ĭ-tĭv

possession pə-zĕsh′ən

possessive pə-zĕs′ĭv

predicate prĕd′ĭ-kĭt

prefix prē′fĭks′

preposition prĕp′ə-zĭsh′ən

prepositional prĕp′ə-zĭsh′ə-nəl

present prĕz′ənt

preterite prĕt′ər-ĭt

principal prĭn′sə-pəl

progressive prə-grĕs′ĭv

pronoun prō′noun′

proper prŏp′ər

question kwĕs′chən

referent rĕf′ər-ənt

reflexive rĭ-flĕk′sĭv

regular rĕg′yə-lər

relative rĕl′ə-tĭv

restrictive rĭ-strĭk′tĭv

rhetorical rĭ-tôr′ĭ-kəl′

root rōōt

run-on rŭn′ŏn′

second sĕk′ənd

sentence sĕn′təns

simple sĭm′pəl

singular sĭng′gyə-lər

speech spēch

splice splīs

split splĭt

stem stĕm

strong strông

subject sŭb′jĕkt′

subjective səb-jĕk′tĭv

subjunctive səb-jŭngk′tĭv

subordinate sə-bôr′dn-ĭt

subordinating sə-bôr′dn-ā′tĭng

suffix sŭf′ĭks

superlative sōō-pûr′lə-tĭv

syntax sĭn′tăks′

tag tăg

tense tĕns

third thûrd

transitive trăn′zĭ-tĭv

understood ŭn′dər-stōōd′

verb vûrb

verbal vûr′bəl

voice vois

weak wēk

word wûrd

yes-no yĕs–nō

zero zîr′ō

PRONUNCIATION KEY

Symbol	Examples	Symbol	Examples
ă	pat	oi	noise
ā	pay	ŏŏ	took
âr	care	ŏŏr	lure
ä	father	ōō	boot
b	bib	ou	out
ch	church	p	pop
d	deed, milled	r	roar
ĕ	pet	s	sauce
ē	bee	sh	ship, dish
f	fife, phase, rough	t	tight, stopped
		th	thin
g	gag	ŭ	cut
h	hat	ûr	urge, term, firm, word, heard
ĭ	pit		
ī	pie, by		
îr	deer, pier	v	valve
j	judge	w	with
k	kick, cat, pique	y	yes
l	lid, needle	z	zebra, xylem
m	mum	zh	vision, pleasure, garage
n	no, sudden		
ng	thing		
ŏ	pot	ə	about, item, edible, gallop, circus
ō	toe		
ô	caught, paw		
ôr	core	ər	butter